MOSTLY TRUE

ALAN MUSKETT MD

Dedication

This collection is dedicated to my many readers and patients who provide constant feedback and support for my particular brand of medical commentary. My first reader is always my wife Pam, who is responsible for the deletion of many inappropriate comments that might have ended my career. My erudite and gracious mother Bess remains my most lasting literary influence. My children Sally, Cathy, and Luke have served as frequent targets for cheap humor. I would like to thank the Billings Gazette and my editor Suzanne Ady for the opportunity and the freedom to present my work.

Acknowledgements

Illustrations by Meghan and Carol Spielman
Photography by Paul Ruhter
Design by Accent Print Shop

About the Author 〜〜〜〜〜〜〜〜〜

Dr. Alan Muskett, son of Bess and Al Muskett, is a native of Missoula, Montana, graduating from Sentinel High School in 1975, which really wasn't all that long ago. He received a degree in English Literature from Montana State University, then an MD from the University of Washington. He did a general surgery residency at the University of Utah, followed by a residency in cardiovascular surgery at Washington University in St. Louis, Mo. In 1991, he began private practice in Billings, Mt. and over the next twelve years did cardiac, thoracic, and vascular surgery. In 2003, he began a residency in plastic surgery at the University of Mississippi, and returned to Billings in 2005, joining Dr. Steve Grosso at Billings Plastic Surgery. Over his careers in Billings, he has written features for the Health Section of the Billings Gazette. Selections of those columns, as well as some other pieces, comprise this collection.

Introduction

It started out conventionally. In the early 1990s, as I was beginning my career as a cardiovascular surgeon, I began writing informative, sober articles on things like carotid artery blockages and techniques of coronary bypass. Over time, I started inserting slightly more editorial and personal reflections on medical topics. I found that readers responded most to humorous or somewhat offbeat approaches to usually serious topics.

You would think that patients would prefer grown-up doctors, but I find that most feel more comfortable with their physicians and other providers if they see them as human and approachable. We all have basically the same human desires, impulses, weaknesses, and problems. If a common language of humanity and humor can be established, then important information can be communicated. If I can entertain my readers, then they might let me preach a bit.

We tend to think of humor or laughter as somewhat inconsequential. Comedic movies never win Academy Awards. But after countless conversations with readers, I am convinced that there is a deeply therapeutic effect of laughter, of indulging in silliness. It also serves to strip away the mysticism and fear that surrounds illness and medicine.

I hope you enjoy this collection of pieces that have appeared in the Billings Gazette over the years, and some that, because of their length, were published elsewhere. They are grouped loosely by general topics, but they are all steeped in the gratitude I have for a job that lends meaning to my life, and the privilege to write about it.

Contents

Chapter 1
Weird Diseases

We tend to think of diseases as things like infection or cancer or conditions that involve spots. But there are afflictions that are dark and debilitating that must be brought to light; things involving golf clubs and insanity.

~~~~~~~~~~~~~~~~~~~~~~~~~~

Midlife Male Insanity (MMI)

It's officially an epidemic. As more and more cases occur, the numbers dwarf the *E. coli* outbreak in Europe. Yet little is written on this insidious condition despite the fact that the devastation wrought is splashed all over the news media. Like many dirty secrets it is hushed away, too toxic to talk about. Maybe you or a family member have been affected and don't want to experience the shame of exposure.

As one of your fearless health reporters, however, I feel it is time to rip the shroud off this scandalous sewer and skewer it with the spotlight of truth.

I am speaking of MMI. Not familiar with MMI? We doctors purposely use abbreviations and acronyms, so that you will have to pay us to tell you what they are. For the nominal cost of this newspaper, however, I will tell you. MMI is Midlife Male Insanity.

More fulminant than the most aggressive cancer, more devastating than a heart attack, more catastrophic in its consequences than wrecking your pickup, MMI is sweeping across the social, political, and social landscapes faster than your teenager can steal your cell phone upgrade.

Otherwise talented, successful, intelligent, fully actualized men go ape, berserk, batty, bonkers—and that's only the As and Bs.

Bill Clinton was impeached and nearly convicted for an assignation with an intern his daughter's age, who was not Marilyn Monroe, not even close. From a strictly Male Pig perspective, if it *were* Marilyn Monroe, a lot of men would condemn the President in front of their wives, then secretly say "what choice did the dude have?", but Monica? Really?

Tiger Woods, Brett Farve, Kobe Bryant. Hundreds of millions of dollars, literally, for tawdry romps with women way less hot than their wives. Elliot Spitzer, Governor of New York, Arnold Schwarzenegger, Governator of California, that third world country south of Oregon. Then the recent texting business with the unfortunately named Anthony Weiner, guys taking pictures of their nether anatomy and inflicting the images on cyberspace. To top it off, that French finance minister got tangled up with a maid in New York, costing him what looked like a clear shot at Prime Minister. Big deal. France hasn't made the playoffs since Napoleon.

MMI doesn't just affect the celebrity class. You all know someone who's slipped his clutch. Husband, father, brother, friend, co-worker—I'll bet it took you two seconds to think of someone who is just as big an idiot as these guys.

I pored over all the medical literature trying to find the cause for MMI—tumor, hormones, head trauma, environmental poisoning, etc... There was one lame study from the Mayo Clinic about declining testosterone levels in aging males. I don't think declining testosterone is the issue here.

Since the literature is so sparse, I've decided to describe the condition myself as MMI. I would call it Muskett's Disease, as a lot of pioneers name diseases after themselves, but that moniker is already assigned to the condition of being obsessed with full displacement trawler yachts. Plus I am exceedingly modest.

Anyway, from what I've been able to determine, the condition is multi-factorial. It seems to be a combination of insatiable ego, rampant insecurity, a desire to dominate, hormonal warp-drive, and the moral code and judgment of a junkyard dog. Speaking of dogs, by far the most useful description of this condition and its treatment came from the dog training literature, where it was suggested that a low level electrical shock be delivered to the dog's collar whenever he pounced upon an unsuspecting female, or actually even *thought* about such an act. It might be a breakthrough if applied in the treatment of sports figures or politicians.

Another treatment modality is to accept the male need for variety, confront the reality of dalliance, and incorporate the idea of affairs into a contemporary committed relationship. Blasphemy? Hear me out. Simply have the affair with your wife. Their rates are generally very reasonable (a half or a third of the expected flowers and jewelry), they'll count breakfast at the Muzzle Loader without the kids as romantic canoodling, and a second honeymoon in Vegas for the NASCAR races will probably pass muster. You don't have to worry about your gut either; they already know you're sucking it in.

What I did find in my research was that one of the most profound influences on our health is the number and quality of our relationships. Connected people have fewer illnesses and live longer. Relationships are not accidental, they are intentional, and they are hard work.

Repudiation of our selfish, narcissistic, or biologically greedy impulses is not repressive. These things rupture relationships that literally keep us alive. Look at Tiger or Arnold, dumped by a couple of classy women. They look like lonely jerks. Perhaps the best thing you can do for your health is not aspirin, yoga, Lipitor, or fish oil, but rather to build the personal relationships that will keep you alive and happy. As banal as commitment and fidelity may appear, you are pretty boring yourself, so get over it.

I'm not saying I'm thrilled with the collar, but they do come in many colors to match my scrubs.

The Plague That Never Leaves

The threat of some nasty disease that will wipe us all out has been around since the first human smoke-signaled in sick for a mammoth hunt. The bubonic plague took out a third of Europe in the Middle Ages. Small pox decimated the native peoples of the Americas. Some of you remember the terror of polio. In 1918 fifty million people worldwide, including seven hundred thousand Americans, died of a virulent flu virus. In 1930 there was a scare over parrot fever that caused the neck wringing of thousands of innocent parrots. The modern HIV/AIDS situation revived fears of a complex virus with unstoppable features.

So what to think of the swine flu? There are reports from other countries about infections and the swift demise of the victims. How many movies have you seen where a virus wipes out the whole world except for a brooding hunky male with an appealing dog and a hot single mom with a precocious and adorable kid? Being none of those, I wondered about how bad the swine flu could be. I asked two local infectious disease experts about the behavior of swine flu in this area.

Dr. Cam Saberhagen of the Billings Clinic told me that the swine flu virus is of concern due to its relatively novel genetic makeup. Because it is different from other viruses, we don't recognize it as well immunologically. However, the cases she has seen have been relatively mild, perhaps indicating some genetic evolution. Dr. Fred Kahn of the Respiratory Center has had a similar experience, stating that he was recently in New York City mingling with ten million other people with no masks on and he wasn't sweating it.

I took the opportunity to ask these experts about other concerns I had, more personal in nature. I am a victim of Chronic Relapsing Spring Fever (CRSF), which the medical establishment has suppressed and covered up for years. The symptoms are restlessness, frequent sighing, and an unusual interest in boating and fishing magazines. I asked Dr. Saberhagen about this very serious illness—is it a virus, a bacterium, a new super bug? "It is likely a virus found in persons with an aversion to work," she replied, "and it is also associated with maturational arrest." I thought Dr. Kahn might be more sympathetic, so I asked him about the chest pain and shortness of breath that occurs with CRSF. "More like old and out of shape than some bug, " was his comment. No wonder my disability insurance carrier won't return my calls.

Rat studies have shown that when populations increase, communicable diseases increase also. Rat studies don't always correlate with human biology, because rats don't shoot, nuke, car bomb, stab, or poison each other. But that aside, we must be increasingly aware of our vulnerability to evolving infectious pathogens. If your kids are in sports, be meticulous about clean gear, showering, prompt treatment of wounds, and hand washing. There are a lot of nasty resistant staph infections around sports. Any type of wound, body fluid, runny nose, cough, etc., can lead to transmission, so get everyone on board with hygiene. People like Dr. Saberhagen and Dr. Kahn have convinced me to wash my hands about fifty times a day while at work, the result being my skin is reptilian and my fingernails have dissolved.

Of course you are a zillion times more likely to be killed by a car, a cigarette, a cheeseburger, a fifth of JD, or an indignant spouse than you are by some exotic disease. But those are old, tiresome sermon topics. It is the Spring Fever that thrums the strings of your soul; the warm breezes and lilac scents, the ice breaking up on the lake, a snowy mountain against a stark blue sky—a fever not of disease but of a yearning for rebirth, of green shoots and dewy blossoms, of anticipated joy.

Fear and Fear Itself

Like many families, we've had some great times in the national parks in Montana. We have an adorable picture of Cathy feeding a hot dog to a grizzly bear, and the one of Sally sitting on a buffalo is just precious. This summer, we decided to hike around Many Glacier, which necessitated a trip over the Going-To-The-Sun-Highway. I have sucked it up and driven this Glacier Park mainstay many times before, but as I age, my acrophobia (stark raving fear of heights) has gotten worse rather than better. This time, I got in the back seat with a big pillow over my head while my wife drove, she of course loving it, the stentorian control freak reduced to a pathetic puddle of gelatinous panic.

I've tried reconditioning, stern lectures to myself, whatever, none of it works—and my acrophobia gets worse. It baffles me. I'm not exactly a wuss, I don't think—I've taken eleven medical board exams, I did 2,000 open heart surgeries, and survived 14 years of medical training, but I can barely handle a two story stairwell. So what can I say to people who are terrified of events medical? That they are big fat chickens?

I did some moonlighting in an ER in Utah when I was doing some research as a surgical resident. It was a small ER, and I usually worked with Ramona, who was like a Mormon Jewish mother to me. She had eight of her own children, and she also took great care of me. She fed me, told me what to do when I didn't know, and mightily smote anyone who messed with me. One night this 17-year-old kid came in with a relatively minor laceration, acting all cool with his equally cool girlfriend. Once I pulled out the needles he started thrashing around, sort of shoving me, whining like a little baby. I was flummoxed. Ramona sidled over, put the vice grips on his arm, and said "shoot him up." She then told the kid that in no universe she was acquainted with did a man behave that way, especially in front of a woman, and then told the girl to dump this gerbil and find herself a man properly equipped. The message Ramona conveyed to me was that one's behavior in a medical setting has a heavy cultural context.

Fear is a big deal in medicine. Fear keeps you from getting something checked out because you don't want to find out you have cancer. The cliché is that we most fear the unknown, but the known can be pretty bad too. The lump in the breast, the blood in the stool, or the pains in the chest suggest something bad, a place we don't want to visit. So maybe it is best to wait and see.

6

Fear of pain is what allows things to grow and spread, to close off, to go from manageable to disastrous. Who wants the shot, the tube, the mask, the bundling of one's corpus into a gyrating machine that will interrogate your very soul? As long as you don't go to the doctor or have that test things are OK, aren't they?

Does this sound familiar? So what do you do to get around it? First, embrace your inner big fat chicken. Identify someone you trust who is annoyingly pesky, and tell them about your delinquent mammogram or colonoscopy or physical, and then they will likely hound you until you do it. You need outside pressure or you will procrastinate until you are a psychotic wreck.

Next, be honest with the provider (I'm still getting used to that word) who will be doing any procedure on you. The difference between patients is huge, but you have to let us know. I recently did an otoplasty (repair of prominent ears) on a 12-year-old girl. Not only did she not want general anesthesia, she refused sedation because she wanted to watch the whole thing. "I want to see the cuts", she said, so I showed her the first incision with a mirror. "No", she said, "I want to see the incision while you are doing it." After I had done the initial set back of the ears, she suggested I take another couple millimeters off the right one. On the other hand, I recently had an adult practically discombobulate during a tiny mole removal. If we know ahead of time, we can do a lot of things to help. We have great new anesthetic creams to take the sting out of shots. It is reasonable in some cases to do some sedation with pills ahead of time. For bigger cases like facelifts, rhinoplasties, facial lasers, brows and eyelids, we do a combination of oral and IV sedation.

Patients are often reluctant to mention their anxieties because it is embarrassing. I've frozen up a couple of times on hikes when there were big drop-offs and I just couldn't proceed, and it was embarrassing. I've learned, though, that it is better to be up front ahead of time about that sort of thing than be put in an acutely uncomfortable position. We all have our Kryptonite, that peculiar vulnerability, that fear that is as inexplicable as it is debilitating. In many cases, that fear involves medical stuff. That's cool, just own it, but don't let it kill you.

Franklin Roosevelt said "All we have to fear is fear itself." Personally I think that is one of the silliest quotes of all time. Am I the only one out there that believes that? I think we should fear plunging off the side of that Going-to-the-Sun highway and being crushed like a can of Bud Lite. But I have to survive long enough to get that picture of my son spray-painting his initials on the big horn sheep.

Men Are Neglected

I recently attended the YWCA's Salute to Women, a tribute to a group of remarkably talented and productive local women. It was a moving evening, but I couldn't help but think "What about the men?" In health care, all you hear about these days are women's health initiatives. There are seminars on women and heart disease, special floors in hospitals for women, women's runs, you name it.

The men's floor in the hospital is between the trash incinerator and the morgue.

My wife contends that the entirety of human history is one long Salute to Men. With such backward attitudes, it is easy to see how men's health issues have been neglected. From a public perspective, about all we men have going for us is prostate cancer. About 186,000 men get prostate cancer each year, and 28,000 die. Screening for prostate cancer includes examination (that's right, the one with the glove) and a blood test called PSA (Prostatic Specific Antigen). Make sure to ask your doctor about these studies, but don't hold your breath waiting for the Prostate Run for Life or a Prostate Wristband. The only other high profile condition for men is "ED", short for erectile dysfunction, which based on all the ads during the Master's, results from playing too much golf.

My purpose today is to educate you regarding the many conditions affecting men that aren't discussed, due to colloquial attitudes and fear of embarrassment. Breaking down barriers is the key to understanding.

Lateral epicondylitis, commonly referred to as "tennis elbow", happens commonly to men as a result of overuse of toilet brushes. Frequent and sometimes even compulsive cleaning with circular brushes leads to this painful elbow inflammation. Often associated with this is another painful malady called de Quervain's tenosynovitis, which is when tendons to the thumb become inflamed. This most frequently happens with changing the empty toilet paper rolls over and over. Rest is only cure for these problems.

Lumbar strain, or low back pain, occurs when men are loading and unloading the washer and dryer while not using proper body mechanics. Frankly, I think women are often insensitive to this malady. I know that you take this commotion in the laundry room for granted, but once in a while step in and remind him to bend at the knees and not at the waist. And while you are at it, ladies, it wouldn't hurt you to get up a few minutes earlier so he doesn't have to wait to make the bed.

I was personally affected by this next condition, contact dermatitis. This is a malady where your skin breaks out when it comes in contact with a certain substance. In my case, it was the adhesive they use on the sticky strips on Pampers. They must use the same glue on Huggies and the rest of them, because they all did the same thing to my hands. I was devastated. I was unable to share in this most critical of bonding experiences, diaper changing. I think that is why my daughters have struggled in chemistry.

I hope to suit up and lead the fight for men's health, just as soon as someone fills up my sock drawer.

Golf Can Be Dangerous

Despite years of school and residency and practice, I am always encountering holes in my medical knowledge. For instance, I didn't realize how dangerous a game golf could be.

The image of the world's greatest golfer, some say the world's greatest athlete, lying semi-conscious and shoeless on the street outside his home startled me. His face begged a "replace your divots" sign. The back window of his Escalade was missing, and a three iron lay nearby trying to look innocent. I figured that after his successful ACL repair, Tiger was more likely to fall off his yacht than suffer a serious occupational injury. Since this represented a clear hole in my knowledge base, I decided to consult experts.

Dr. Jim Elliot, an orthopedic surgeon, told me he has twice treated golfers who have had open fractures (that's the bone sticking through the skin kind--yuck) of both bones in the lower legs. One wouldn't think that stepping out of a golf cart would lead to such a violent injury, but if the cart is still speeding along, and if you have had north of six frosty Buds in as many holes, the risk profile changes.

I then spoke to Rachel Warren, a former Billings Central and Rocky Mountain College champion golfer, to get a female pro's perspective on the situation. There are allegations that Tiger's wife Elin may have used a golf club as a facilitative device in their martial dialogue, specifically the aforementioned three iron. "Certainly club selection is always important," Ms. Warren opined. "I might have chosen a sand wedge as it has a nice sharp leading edge. It is a relatively short club and not hollow and broad like a driver. It should get her into the car quickly." My thought was that it would likely leave a divot as well.

Once Tiger was done with his CT scans and plastic surgeon and I'm guessing a dentist as well, the fun started. Your face is a throbbing eggplant, public voyeurism verges on hysteria, and your prenup just went up 70 million. Every red-blooded American male wannabe jock in the country, who has wanted to *be* Tiger, looks at side by side photographs of his Vegas playpals (rather, shall we say, professional-looking) and his Norwegian wife (smokin' hot) and says "Dude, seriously, you got more than your sand wedged." So yes, golf can lead to some major complications.

My golf expert, Rachel, said it best: "I think I would rather be Tiger than Elin right now. His wounds will hurt less and heal more quickly." Every doctor sees patients who are decidedly unwell without a blood test or an x-ray that is abnormal. A broken heart doesn't register on an EKG, but it can cripple you and kill you just as much as any tumor.

I got a call at five this morning about a guy who got punched on the side of the head. His ear was shredded, and while I was putting the parts back together, I pondered how differently we regard physical versus emotional assault. This ear would be expensive and painful, but he'll get over it in a while. He can, if he wants, file charges or sue the guy. If you promise 'til death do us part, forsaking all others, then betray that trust, you can inflict a wound more lacerating and devastating than any punch or gun. It is not an inconsequential health issue. I would be very surprised if you or someone you know hasn't been really damaged in that way. I don't care if a single Tiger wants to win a purple jacket for being the Master horndog, but you can't be Mr. Gatorade/Nike/AMEX/adorable daddy at the same time and not hurt people.

As surely as we strap our kids in car seats, drive prudently to protect our friends, and feed, clothe, and shelter our families, this salacious little episode reminds us that our behaviors and commitments matter a great deal to the health of the people around us. What does a healthy body do for you if your soul is merely wistful ashes?

Much of health has to do, of course, with prevention. Just in case, I have locked away the golf clubs, chainsaws, sharp garden tools, and tin snips in the garage. Like I said, your knowledge is never complete.

Chapter 2
Getting Personal

There are intensely personal issues common to all of us—guilt, our responses to pressure and adversity, aging, and the fears we have regarding illness in ourselves and in our loved ones. That we share these concerns makes them more bearable, and that we share them makes them interesting material for both introspection and fun.

~~~~~~~~~~~~~~~~~~~~

The Good Angel vs. the Bad Angel

Our predisposition is to view the scuffle between good and evil as macroscopic—ideologically fervent, furtive killers with bombs versus the egalitarian professors of intellectual freedom. Far greater, however, is the battle raging between our own ears. Therein lies our consciousness, the playing field where our noble, altruistic theses cross swords with our selfish, venal, and hedonistic darkness.

Today, in this exclusive, never seen before inside look at the process that is your medical care, I will expose this epic struggle in the form of a series of conversations. The participants are the patient, a good angel, (naturally residing on the surgeon's right shoulder), and a bad angel (on the left.)

Patient: "Accidents happen, I have the worst luck."

Good Angel: "We'll do everything we can to help you through this."

Bad Angel: *"Dude. Accident? Seriously? Hundred and twenty miles an hour down the wrong side of the road. Missed a turn, flipped, rolled three times, ejected (no seatbelt of course) and all you get is a mashed face and two femur fractures. Besides the blood alcohol of .223, the positives on your tox screen ran two pages. The only accident here is that Darwin's natural selection took a night off and allowed you to survive.*

Patient: "There's no way I can afford these antibiotics."

Good Angel: "We'll put you in contact with an prescription assistance program."

Bad Angel: *"Nice IPhone, is that the new 4s? Oh, and those Camels in your pocket, they are running $6.15 a pack now. Your intake form lists a pack-and-a-half a day, so that's nine bucks a day, times thirty, so two hundred seventy bucks a month for cigarettes. So that generic Cipro I gave you is too expensive at thirteen bucks. So when I bill you for that broken jaw, which fake address should I use?*

Patient: "My weight has nothing to do with it."

Good Angel: "There are certainly many factors involved."

Bad Angel: *"No, of course not. No reason your knees shouldn't be able to pack around 350 pounds. No reason your pancreas, built for a gymnast, shouldn't be able to handle the 8500 calories you slurp down every day. No reason your heart, a thirty-horse outboard, shouldn't be able to push a supertanker across the ocean.*

What keeps the bad angel quiet, in my case, is that I am just as big an idiot as anyone else. I like my cholesterol, booze, and couch time too much to be the healthiest I could be. I think we all find a place on the spectrum from delicious depravity to annoying asceticism that allows us comfort.

But a society, and particularly a medical system, without some degree of judgment will fail. I have the libertarian belief than you can do whatever you want with your health and body as long as it doesn't hurt others *and as long as you personally are willing to pay for it.* If you want the taxpayers or other policyholders to pay for your screw-ups, then you abrogate that freedom. For those of you with college students lingering in those lavishly expensive day care centers, you know what I'm talking about.

Good Angel: "I can't believe he writes this oafish, unprofessional, juvenile tripe about a noble profession."

Bad Angel: "He leaves most of the good stuff out."

Aging Gracefully—Or Not

I have decided that I will not become rich and famous going to the ER to see people who have fallen off their motorcycles. It seems like it is the doctors who write books are the ones who schmooze on Oprah's couch. It also seems that the best selling books are ones about money, weight loss, or some sort of personal improvement ("Dialoguing with Your Sensitive Inner Carnivore"). So, I figured, why not combine *all* those ideas into one book, "Dr. Muskett's Guide to Empowerment, Riches, and Rock Hard Abs", or maybe "Peace at Home in a Mansion on Your Buns of Steel." OK, the title needs a little work

The world has changed. Duh. What I mean is that we boomers (yes, you new AARP targets) can't come to grips with conventional aging. We think by going to Rolling Stones concerts, wearing lycra biking shorts, and having more gigabytes than the next guy that we are still young and cool. Of course, we aren't. The point is not to care. If you are a typical parent, you see your children as more absorbed, less respectful, and generally more indolent than yourself. What a perfect way to get even, then, by embarrassing your children with your music, clothing, politics, or yourself in general.

Aging gracefully is out. Spend that inheritance. Kids eyeing your stash? Spend it on cosmetic surgery! Hang around and be a burden. This 4th of July I played three hours of hoops with my teenage daughters and a bunch of 18 to 23 year old guys Later that day, as I lay near death on the couch, I reflected on how awesome it was, just to be in the way. Now the only reason they let me play is because I told them I would cut off their college money if they didn't. This is termed Healthy Communication. My next book "Coercion and Extortion—Strategies of Effective Parenting", will be out soon.

So what is the secret to being a long-term burden to your children? Probably first and foremost is be smart. Actually, you don't have to be smart. Just don't be stupid. One thing I am seeing a lot of lately are energetic boomers getting motorcycles. That is fine, but they get these great big bikes and don't get the training to handle them. It is often simple mistakes that rob people of decades of useful life. More and more people are getting melanoma, and that stuff is nasty. Yeah, we all grew up sun bunnies, but it's time to repent hard.

Keep the weight off. There isn't a condition or disease or anything that is improved by excess weight. Cancer, diabetes, cardiovascular disease, arthritis, all the big stuff is less likely if you aren't heavy. So how, you ask? This is the diet section of the book. The secret is.....don't eat anything. Seriously. At thirty, you can have dessert once a week. At forty, you can maintain stable weight by eating cottage cheese and dry lettuce once a day. At fifty, if you eat a celery stick, you will gain 5 pounds. One slice of lean turkey breast requires 16 hours on the treadmill. And light beer? Put one drop of lemon juice in a glass of that gray water from your RV and it tastes about as good. I am truly amazed at how much less you can eat and how much more you have to exercise as you age. I do think that the low carbohydrate diets, minus all the big time grease, work well. Whatever you choose, life from 50 to 85 will be a lot less complicated if you get rid of the excess weight.

In England, where there is a national health care system, the government did a study to see just how much smoking was costing the health system. They found that smokers, over the course of their life, used *fewer* pounds sterling in health care costs, because they were, well, dead. Hmmm.

Twice a week I attend Tumor Boards, which are meetings of all health care providers involved in cancer treatment. Man, it's pretty scary listening to all these case presentations about people with cancer, especially this week when everyone was 51, which is my calendar (not emotional or, you know, *real*) age. A few pearls I've picked up for my own use. Patient had mammograms—earlier cancer with fewer lymph nodes involved. No mammogram—bigger tumor with more lymph nodes. Colon cancer—found with a screening colonoscopy—often completely curable. Found when you turn yellow with liver involvement—very bad. Now I am a complete hypocrite because I am 51 and you are supposed to get colonoscopy at 50. I will do it this fall, but I do not relish the idea, as the visual imagery of that very long black tube going...you get the idea. But that is an example of a simple mistake that can kill you.

Pick your parents wisely. A lot of health stuff is genetic. Too late to pick your parents? Then pay attention to what runs in your family. If you had a parent or sibling with a heart attack, then get those cholesterols checked and stress tests done. Cancer also has a big hereditary component, so mammograms, prostate blood tests, colonoscopy, and a careful history taken by your provider are all potentially life saving. Think about a football game. What determines who wins or loses? Is it something complicated like throwing a seam route to the hot receiver when the defense was in a Cover Two? No. It is because someone dropped a ball at the wrong time. Life is like that. Your health is like that. Do the simple stuff, don't make the dumb mistakes. It helps greatly to be lucky, too, because some disease and conditions are beyond our control.

So if you are wise enough to shuck out 29.95 for my book, you can look forward to a very small funeral, as you will have outlived all the wimps. There will be no tears, because everyone will be glad you finally croaked. Your annoyed offspring will have you cremated and stuffed in a Folger's can, because your last breath and last penny were at the same moment in time. And it was good.

16

Stuff You Don't Say

I was sitting in one of those remarkably sterile waiting rooms, at an auto service place, when I overheard a startling conversation. A thirtyish mom, holding a sizable and rather churlish three-year-old, noticed another customer, a mere slip of a girl, who was obviously very pregnant.

"You look like you carrying a big 'un", the mom said between wrestling moves designed to restrain the bored toddler. "Frankie here was near ten pounds, and he split me like a watermelon fell off a pickup truck."

The poor girl paled, and in a panic I tried to retrieve my baby delivering skills from thirty years ago.

Another vignette—recently a patient told me that she had come to see me for facial rejuvenation—laser, facelift, whatever—because her mother said "My dear, how you have aged."

Help me out here. In what universe, on what planet far, far away, could those comments possibly be construed as kind, helpful, or affirming in any way?

I feel it my solemn duty, as the unofficial, unelected, and unauthorized medical etiquette maven of the Health Section, to provide you with the Guide To Stuff You Don't Say To People In A Medical Context.

Remember, as in many things in life, most in fact, It's Not About You. It is about the sick or pregnant or afflicted. Do not, for instance, go to a hospital or see someone if you are a Major Wuss. Example: many times in my career I have seen well meaning souls come into the ICU to visit, then burst into tears or say "Oh My God." Besides being blasphemous, patients, anybody in fact, do not want to hear OMG when being looked at. That means you look terrible and are about to die or something worse. Also, do not say "you are looking good." No one looks good in the hospital unless they are on "Days of Our Lives" and have just had two hours of makeup and hair. The patient clearly knows you are lying and won't believe anything else. Do not say "you're going to make it" because the patient will be begin to wonder if "making it" is in fact in doubt.

I had the perfect hospital visit after a procedure once—one of my home boys came into the room railing about some political problem at work, just like he always does really, then suddenly grew serious. "Look," he said, "are they going to give you a bunch of Percocet to go home? If they do, don't be a pig and eat them all yourself." Perfect.

Fact—No one cares about your operation, your uncle who died after a routine bypass, your neighbor who got a terrible infection after breast reconstruction, or your niece whose baby was born with a dorsal fin and two flippers. How many stitches you had, how long you labored, how bad you were stove up, what your sister-in-law's father's doctor said was the worst one he'd ever seen—can it.

Do not tell someone they look tired, old, haggard, aged, saggy, or fat. If someone is tired, old, haggard, aged, saggy, or fat, they know it and don't need to be told.   One patient told me that she had come in because her significant other had characterized her breasts as "two hard-fried eggs about to slide to the floor." Do not say that. No one wants to hear any of those things. Some would argue those are expressions of concern and interest. Figure out another way to express concern besides telling them they look lousy—like watching their kid, doing an errand, or accidentally running over their child support-owing ex-husband so they can collect on an old life insurance policy.

What should you do?   Here's the answer, from a song by Allison Kraus

The smile on your face lets me know that you need me
There's a truth in your eyes sayin' you'll never leave me
The touch of your hand says you'll catch me if ever I fall
You say it best when you say nothing at all

Illness is frightening, renders an uncharacteristic feeling of vulnerability, and creates an urge for the familiar and safe.

Most of all, we don't want to face it alone. When someone in your life is ill, or is down somehow, don't talk too much. Your presence is the only necessary message—the expiation of our fears comes from sharing with an empathetic listener.

Lay hands upon someone in need. Touch is a big part of my practice. I have probably helped more people with my bare hands than with a scalpel or suture. Certainly Jesus had the power to heal people from across the parking lot, but he always laid hands on people, for a reason.

Let a suffering person know, once, that you are available to help, but don't hover—let them tell you what they need, or just anticipate it.

Finally, did I tell you about my colonoscopy? The doc said he had never seen anything like it, why the thing was...........(wait, I wasn't done.)

When It's Your Fault

You've got to love excuses. Excuses are an unappreciated art form.

"Son, go outside and get a log for the fire."

"But Dad, I don't have the right shoes."

Excuses evolve with time, like any great societal barometer. Take the modern politician, a married father professing family values. He is caught on video with a transgender entertainment professional, clad only in a costume with strong leather and metal motifs. At the tearful press conference, he admits to "being human, and humans make mistakes." Right. A mistake. Later it turns out he has made 146 of these mistakes. Could have happened to anybody.

Unfortunately, the maestros, the true geniuses of excuses, play to a relatively small audience. These are surgeons who have a perfectly valid reason for every complication they have. The patient was too fat, too skinny, too old, too young, alcoholic, smoker, you name it. I had bad help, worse instruments, the music was bad. In training, I worked with a professor who could have found a way to blame me for the assassination of Lincoln.

The problem with excuses is that even if someone buys your lame offering, you can't ultimately fool yourself.

As a kid, I dreamed of performing big, dramatic operations that would save lives. Unlike most childhood dreams, mine actually happened. I've had the privilege of reaching deep into the earth and snatching people out of the grave.

Childhood dreams tend to be one-dimensional. You don't realize that with great thrills there can be devastating losses. I have made decisions, or have done procedures in a way that have cost people their lives.

Sure, you can say that they were sick, or that they wouldn't have been on that operating table if all were well, but then we're back to excuses, aren't we? If I had done something different, or better, they might still be alive.

Some of you may have done something similar. Maybe you made a mistake in a car, or a child drowned on your watch. Many men got others killed in combat. There are industrial accidents, boats, four wheelers, and countless other lurking dangers.

Maybe you didn't kill someone, but rather did something irrevocable in a relationship, or at work. You ruined a marriage by cheating. Wrecked your business through some stupid mistake. Said something, didn't say something; did something, didn't do something. You've done something that with all your heart and might and soul you want to take back, but can't.

So how have I survived? The sooner you acknowledge your culpability the better. Rather than say "well, she was a morbidly obese diabetic smoker with a bad heart anyway", you have to accept that you operated on that person and that person died. Those are the facts. It is pointless to get into the self-flagellating "I'm a bad person, a bad surgeon, a killer, etc."

Early and objective acceptance of your role in the incident prevents the grinding, subterranean anxiety that will eventually destroy you if you deny your responsibility. Own up to it, but don't beat yourself up.

You don't "get over" a bad loss. I think that is a major misconception. What you can do is give that loss a place in your life that is tolerable. In order to learn, to get better, a surgeon has to remember what has happened and why. He or she can forgive himself or herself eventually, but they must remember. You can't help others if you are wallowing in the soft, warm, luxuriant blanket of self-pity. Don't punish yourself, but do make yourself get better.

Heartache is a known risk of human existence—it moves into our lives without warning, like a mangy mutt appearing in the rain on our doorstep. There are times in our lives when we forced to make a place, sometimes permanently, for an unwanted presence. It is the cost for the moments of inexpressible joy and exquisite connection that define our lives.

"Go get another log."

"But dad, it is warm enough in here already, and you are producing greenhouse gases."

That kid will make a great surgeon.

Pressure

Pressure pushing down on me
Pressing down on you

The rock group Queen played in front of audiences that at times exceeded 100,000.
Is that pressure?

You're down by one point. Two free throws. No time remaining.
Is that pressure?

A young couple hands you their only child to be taken to surgery. Is that pressure?

My patients are curious about the "pressure" and "stress" associated with medical practice. I finished medical school nearly thirty years ago, and in that time I've been nervous, anxious, terrified, scared, filled with dread, nauseated, panicked, petrified, and a few other terms unsuitable for the newspaper. I've wondered at times if I'd just start on fire or blow up. So what have I learned?

You can place two people in exactly the same situation and one will panic. For another, it's "no problem." There really aren't stressful situations so much as there are stressful responses. My cardiac surgery training program was Screamers Central, sixteen faculty members who all sounded like they needed a diaper change. When I got to Billings, Steve Hubbard and Tim Dernbach taught me to do a valve and three bypasses in three hours while never raising their voices, saving their breath instead to discuss whether walnut or maple made better cabinets.

Stress is a simple mathematical formula—take the job you have to do, then divide it by your ability to do it. A big job divided by a lack of talent spiced with insecurity equals big stress. A big job in the hands of a confident and skilled operator is, in the words of one of my supremely arrogant mentors, "just another chance to look good."

How to deal with pressure? Self-knowledge is critical. I thought I wanted to do pediatric hearts until I worked with a surgical genius. Even this maestro took some brutal shots operating on these kids, and I knew if it was bad for him, I would be miserable. As Clint said in the Second Chapter of Dirty Harry (Magnum Force) "A man's got to know his limitations." Yeah, pride goeth before a fall, but it also goeth before an ulcer or a heart attack too.

Getting better is the best pressure relief there is. Each year of my practice has been more enjoyable, as my skills and experience increase. I read, go to meetings, take courses, and watch other surgeons. If you make a mistake, own it, rather than blaming someone else. An old surgical adage is "forgive yourself, but don't forget the lesson."

Prepare for pressure. As a junior in high school, I smoked everyone in the 880-yard run, that is, until the state track meet, when I choked away a championship. The same year I won a state oratory contest, then went to the national contest where the first prize was thirty large. I could barely squeak out my speech. Taking the heat is a learned process. Recovering from failure is a learned skill. I should have an honorary PhD from Tight Collar University.

My daughter cared for a full-term newborn at the University of Washington recently. The child was blue at birth, and for six hours they struggled to establish effective circulation and respiration. When the child finally died, Sally brought the family in to spend time with the child. She then photographed the baby, placed the body in a bag, and rode the elevator to the morgue.

Pretty tough stuff for a 23 year old. "Yeah", she sighed, "but I've played in the Hardin gym on Saturday night." Hardin fans are great—they show up, they're loud, and they don't like Billings Central. She made some mistakes, her coach yelled at her, but she limped to an overtime win. Years later, some of that hard-earned callous paid off.

Perhaps the greatest stress reliever is gratitude. Yeah, I do some tough stuff sometimes, but I have every conceivable advantage. I come from two well educated, loving parents. I am an affluent white male living in the United States, and have good health and a supportive family. Pressure? Try being a single mother with three kids, one with a profound disability. That's pressure. Realizing that lessens the pressure of being one of "Billings Sexiest 50 Plastic Surgeons."

Ah, a life of no pressure, no stress. Floating around on my 58 footer, my bikini clad (although this is under negotiation) First Mate fetching me Coronas (not negotiable, get your own), but you get the idea. Only one tiny problem with a stress free life—there is no growth. The same fire that threatens to consume us also refines and purifies us. The steel of our character, which is forged in suffering, emerges stronger and more flexible.

I'll just put the cooler next to the recliner.

Trouble

Nobody knows the trouble I've seen. And I don't know yours either. We all have troubles, troubles unique to ourselves; but at the end of the troubled day our troubles are pretty much the same. (12 bar blues riff)

There are many categories of trouble—family trouble, medical trouble, money trouble, work trouble—it's a long troubled list.

I think a lot about surgical trouble because I very much wish to avoid it. The principles of avoiding surgical trouble are essentially those of handling life's travails.

To begin with, do not operate on the wrong patient. By this I don't mean cut off the wrong leg or put DD implants in a guy who wants a mole taken off. I mean don't do facelifts or breast reductions on smokers, don't do big elective procedures on whiners, or any procedure on someone in whom the previous 14 procedures have failed. Any surgeon will tell you that about half of their disasters they should have seen coming.

Similarly, if you are a governor or senator, do not dress up in a sheep costume in the presence of prostitutes, all of whom possess camera phones. Young or not-so-young women should not get involved with that sweet, cute guy with the great smile who can't keep a job, but can demolish a cold pack during an evening of Call of Duty III on the X-Box, which he bought with the money he saved by not paying child support. Avoid a stupid decision at the beginning of any procedure and the pain never happens.

Preparation means knowing the surgical technique thoroughly, reviewing xrays and labs, and making sure all your instruments and parts and supplies are in the room before you start. Nothing like losing a couple or three liters of blood during a surgical case and having only one tiny I.V. in place.

Do not go rafting on the Yellowstone River during runoff wearing only cutoffs, no lifejacket, and with the only safety item a cooler of beer. Do not ride a horse you can't handle, or its modern equivalent, the four-wheeler. Do not hit on the girlfriend of a guy twice your size and half as drunk. Do not get on a ladder over the age of 50.

Don't be a hero. I learned that when a patient has three bad heart valves, sometimes the best thing to do is do the worst one or two and get out of there. One of my professors called it the LPO principle—the Live Patient Outcome principle. No one wants to hear your lame excuses, no matter how legitimate, if you bump someone off. Live patients are best.

Do not buy a house or a car or anything you cannot afford or it will slowly kill you. If you can just afford something, you cannot afford it. As with any surgical case, you must leave room for blood loss or a leaky roof. The penalty for overreaching is harsh.

The most immediate surgical trouble is bleeding. Bleeding you can hear or bleeding that hits the ceiling or the wall is really bad. Bleeding where you have to shower and change clothes in the middle of the case is bad too.

In surgery, and in real life, it is rarely the first mistake that kills, but rather the overreaction. It is so tempting with massive bleeding to throw a clamp or a big honking stitch blindly into the mess, hoping for a miracle. This will often make the hole bigger.

How many times do you read about the fatal car crash when the car drifts off the side of the road, the driver snaps out of it, overcorrects, and the car rolls?

So what to do? If you do get in trouble, get control of yourself first. It's okay to panic, but do it calmly. Let the panic wash up and down your tummy and chest, then let it wash out. Breathe deeply and be quiet.

You can't really hurt much by putting your finger in the hole. Most bleeding responds to pressure or a well-placed finger. This buys you time to get your act together and figure out what happened. Another great life/surgery principle—get help. No one thinks less of you for asking for help, but you will be barbequed with hate sauce if you don't.

So when you encounter massive metaphorical bleeding be cool, take your own pulse first, and put a finger in the hole. This often involves keeping your mouth shut, avoiding that verbal clamp or stitch that will cause lasting harm. And by the way, what is more sexy/bad than looking cool under fire? You can be freaking inside, but be sure to look cool.

Most of what I do could be taught to a chimpanzee. What requires four years of med school, ten years of residency, and twenty years of private practice are a few cases a year where all that experience and judgment are required to do the right thing. It is the daily discipline of doing things thoughtfully and carefully, the lifelong orientation of honesty and ethical conduct, and the will to keep getting better that prepares us for those few moments when we really have to get it right.

Just as a point of clarification—the chimpanzee did not write this article. That was last week.

Chapter 3
The Trade of Medicine

Medicine is a trade with workers and tools. So what does surgery have to do with chainsaws, ammo, and teddy bears? Read on.

~~~~~~~~~~~~~~~~~~~~~~~~~~~~~~~~~

Taking Call

"I've run out of ammo, but still have a knife." That's a pretty weird text message to receive, especially at 3 a.m. on a Wednesday morning.

My brother, an ER physician, was having one of those nights. Every drunk, meth-head, crazy, and narc-seeker had selected that time to come to his ER, not to mention a pediatric drowning earlier in the day. As background were the usual assortment of heart attacks, lacerations, and nursing-home residents with perforated colons.

This siege mentality is no doubt responsible for the frequent use of war metaphors by health care providers describing their call experience. "I got killed." "I got nuked." Bombed, shelled, torched—it's a colorful list.

Taking call is certainly not unique to medicine. Many jobs or businesses have a call arrangement—who do you think repairs those power lines when a heavy snow hits on Christmas? Surgeons have to operate any time day or night, but they don't do those operations alone—there is an RN, an OR tech, an OR aide, an anesthesiologist, and all the folks in preop and recovery. The nursing units, not to mention the maintenance, dietary, and supply staffs, are all on a 24 hour clock. But my whining is always more poignant and meaningful than theirs.

A lot of doctors hate call, period. Sleep disruption, no drinking, staying close to town, leaving movies or games, and holidays spent not with your family, but with some unsuccessful pugilist barfing recently guzzled Ripple on your new Christmas sweater.

As doctors age, many begin to fear call, and develop the "yips." One minute you are reading in front of the fire, and a few minutes later someone's teenage child is trying to bleed to death in front of you following a car crash. Imagine you are in your cozy bed, dreaming of 54-foot trawler yachts, and the next minute a starving jungle cat climbs up on your bed. It is that anxious, uncertain, lurking calamity that can wear you out.

Call ultimately, however, is the crucible in which a surgeon is rendered battle ready. (War metaphor, unavoidable). I've told you before of my experiences opening chests emergently, having to put a child on a heart-lung machine *right now*, or placing a pacemaker in a patient with no heart rhythm. My heart was pounding louder than any low-rider subwoofer, and my breathing would have been shallow, but since my throat was clutched shut, it didn't matter. My greatest desire was that some grown-up, experienced doctor would come through the door and save me. But somehow, to my utter astonishment, the job got done. In the tremulous relief that follows, scrubs totally pitted out, shoes and underwear soaked through with blood, this ether of terror and joy incorporates as a voice *"You can do this!"*

Call is how you build your practice. Some plastic surgeons eschew going to the ER—too downscale and grubby. Say you go to the ER to sew up 2-year-old Little Precious, who has a one-centimeter cut on her chin. Little Precious proceeds to kick your teeth out and perforate your one remaining eardrum with screams resembling that of a chain saw encountering a nail. The insurance company will then reimburse you $1.64 for that procedure. A losing deal for sure?

Not so fast. Little Precious is the center of her parent's universe, and you are kind and patient. Her tearfully grateful Yummy Mummy shows up six months later in your office for a breast augmentation, made necessary by the gestational havoc wreaked by Little Precious.

You can take call asleep. A very competent young nurse called me from the ICU at 0200 hours to give me a report on a cardiac surgery patient who was limping a bit. After her recitation of numbers and trends, which I apparently didn't like, I barked "that's enough out of your young lady, you get back into bed right now or you're going to get a big spank." She reported this response to the charge nurse, who told her "give him ten minutes. He'll either call back, or at least he'll be coherent in ten minutes when you call."

The hardest part of call is when you receive information about a patient and you're not sure if you should haul yourself out of a warm cozy bed at 4 a.m. and go see them. Are they bleeding? Septic? Having an MI? Maybe it's OK. Maybe it's not.

The most difficult struggles we face in our lives are with ourselves. We inhabit different universes simultaneously—there is a legal one, where what you can get away with is OK. You can't prove it so I didn't do it. Even if what I did was slimy it isn't illegal. That evidence isn't admissible. My blood alcohol was 0.07.

The moral universe is less forgiving. Did I do the right thing? The answer is just below your ribcage—how does that feel? Is that undulating knot in your gut trying to tell you something? Am I doing my best for my patient, my wife, my children, my business, my practice, my school? Rationalization is what turns a moral argument into a legal one-- a courageous choice, stripped of its humanity, becomes an excuse.

My 54-foot trawler yacht has slipped beneath the waves, knowing I have to get up and drive to the hospital. In the dark, I reach for my shoes and scrubs, trying not to wake my wife.

There is a vague remnant of a guilty dream about threatening to spank someone.

My First Professors

My first surgery professors were three guys named Joe, Adolph, and Tuffy. I was thirteen, an almost certainly illegal employee of a fledgling log home construction company in northwest Montana. There was no OSHA, no hardhats, and no child labor inconveniences. Our outfit was, however, strict about not letting drunks handle chainsaws where they might hurt themselves. Instead, they drove the forklifts.

Joe had a slightly superior attitude toward Adolph and Tuffy— he'd finished eighth grade. All were WWII guys; woodsmen before and after the service, grateful for the slightly less backbreaking work of log home construction as opposed to logging in the woods.

I spent ten summers with them, beginning as a log peeler, and ending as a crew chief just before my second year of med school. They taught me to carve notches and grooves in logs so they fit precisely one on another; so tight the caulking between them was strictly cosmetic. I would display what I thought was a perfect notch, and Adolph would say, "that looks like a (insert at least three profanities, vulgar references, and/or blasphemies) Rottweiler with bad teeth did that notch." This was prior to the invention of self-esteem.

I told them in the beginning, as an eighth grader, that I would be a surgeon, which seemed to amuse them. "You better hope so, because you sure ain't worth a (insert as directed above) at this." They taught me precision, and craftsmanship, and a certain bleak objectivity. If it wasn't good, it wasn't good--do it over. They could file a chain saw so sharp you could shave with it. They taught me that there was a look to quality that was indefinable but undeniably distinct.

I write this during a weekend of smashed bones—jawbones, cheekbones, eye sockets, and foreheads. This is a business of power tools, screws, metal plates—and one really medieval tool you screw into the cheekbone. It has a "joystick" you pull to bring the bone back into place.

One of the patients had totally smashed his face, bled like crazy, and ended up hypothermic by the time he got to the hospital. So the operating room was smoking hot, and I was flashing back to the July days out in the log yard, sweating hard, trying to get things lined up right.

These can be really tough cases—deep holes, terrible swelling, everything bleeding. I was very fortunate to have some good surgical techs helping me—tool guys, seasoned guys, men who know how to fix stuff. Most importantly, they know how to help you fix stuff. In the morning John at the Billings Clinic, and pretty much all Saturday night Bill and Greg at St. Vincent hung with me while we did the business of notches and grooves and plates and screws, bleary hours in an eighty degree room wearing surgical gowns. What would have been perfect would have been to have Adolph peering skeptically into the wound, looking at my fracture reduction, and saying, "my blind grandmother could do better than that and she's been dead twenty years."

I am always struck by the fact that the most relevant experience to my job was not fourteen years of medical education after college but building log houses forty years ago. I remember packing my chainsaw into the yard, a dusty 95 degrees at 2 o'clock in the afternoon, another three hours to go, wondering how I was going to make it. At 3:30 this morning, when I couldn't get the (fill in Adolph's vocab here) screw to hold in the lateral orbital wall, I thought, "pick up your chainsaw and quit whining. You've done this before."

After battles like last night and this morning I am grateful to those in my past who busted on me when I didn't do it right. In a culture of institutionalized victimhood, yapping, and excuses, I really appreciate the women and men next to me in the OR who can load the right screw on the right tool, when I need it, then expose the bone that needs fixing.

I'll bet in one five-hour case we put in more screws than we said words.

Each summer I would tell Joe and Adolph and Tuffy "I'm going to be a surgeon." Tuffy would say "sure, and Raquel Welch is going to climb into my shower any morning now." Finally, in June of 1983, I stopped at the log yard during lunch and presented the boys with my MD diploma from the University of Washington. Tuffy perused it, while I wriggled in triumph, and said "may God have mercy on us all."

Cool Tools

As much as I don't miss the diaphoretic anxieties of finals week, I do miss the delicious release of school's end and the onset of summer break, and the return to the woods of northwest Montana and my job building log homes. I began at 15 peeling logs with a drawknife, and left ten summers later to enter my second year of medical school, when summer vacation is over, forever. Not only do you miss working outside and getting buff from the exercise, a subtle flicker of anxiety suggests you are becoming an Old Person. Old People don't get summer vacation, except for teachers. I would be a teacher if they let me use pepper spray and water cannons and tasers, but I don't see the current PC touchy-feely climate allowing that. My patients are pretty respectful of me, because I am going to put them to sleep and cut on them. I wouldn't antagonize me either.

My technical skills were developed mostly on an ax and a chainsaw. We built custom log homes, where one log had to fit another, so cutting the notches and grooves between the logs was a surgical science. With the right kind of chain, and with the blades finely sharpened, I could essentially sculpt a log with a chainsaw, creating a precise fit to another log. My specialty at the company was repairing logs damaged in transport, foreshadowing a career in breast implants, oops, I mean reconstructive surgery.

I honestly feel I could do most surgical operations with a well functioning chainsaw. I prefer a Stihl with a 24 inch bar.

32

However, the rather provincial and unenlightened operating room personnel at the local surgical facilities have not the faculties to appreciate innovative, outside-the-box trailblazers such as myself, and have resisted my attempts to put such an instrument in the capital budget.

One very useful tool that I do get to use is a cautery pencil, which cuts and coagulates with an electric current. It functions much as a wand, and since many surgeons harbor a secret Harry Potter delusion, it fits right in with wearing special hats. I get to use a carbon dioxide laser, which at lower settings shrinks wrinkles, and at higher settings vaporizes bumps and warts. You never outgrow the desire to blow things up.

Despite having only recent begun to walk upright and use indoor plumbing, orthopedic surgeons have by far the coolest tools. Part of plastic surgery training is spending a few months with the orthopods learning how to do hand surgery, and that was a revelation to me. Big screws with bigger screwdrivers to push them. Drills with bits that they use on oil rigs. Rods. Plates. Reamers. This is Carhartt and Copenhagen stuff. One ton with dualies. I was doing a knee reconstruction case with one of the guys, and the silicone surface wouldn't fit into the metal knee thingee, and out came a sledgehammer. Cool.

The latest fabulous tool is the robot. Both local hospitals have them, of course. The advantage of the robot is the ability to operate in very tight quarters with extreme precision. For instance, when removing a prostate gland, meticulous dissection may spare critical autonomic nerves whose job is, to use the popular parlance of the golf commercial, "erectile function." So maybe each hospital needs to buy two. I don't have any urge to use a robot, though. Much of surgery for me is sensory, prodding and palpating, and robotic surgery seems much like watching someone else make out with your girlfriend. Ultimately the best tools are the oldest and simplest. Ears are for listening. How therapeutic is the unburdening of the soul, the vocalization of embarrassed and sequestered fears. Much of my job, and much more so that of the primary care doctor, is listening, creating a venue for the exposure of wounds both corporeal and spiritual, so that they might be healed, or failing that, addressed with dignity.

Hands are the sensory detectives of diagnosis. (You know how you feel when the glove snaps on, the doctor looking around for the lube) While hands are the tools of investigation and procedures, of stitching and shaping, they are also the tools of reassurance and comfort. One of my favorite Alison Krauss songs "When you say nothing at all" has a line "the touch of your hand says you'll catch me whenever I fall." Illness is like falling; falling from wholeness, falling from confidence, falling from the security of what we know and what we thought we could count on. The steadying hand is as vital as any pill.

The last and greatest tool is the heart. If you can't feel for your patient, even if they are a manipulative drug-seeking sociopathic dirtbag (please see attachment 1, an apology expressing regret for my deeply insensitive and unprofessional remarks, which by no means represent.....) then you need to find another job. To me, the essence of professionalism, whether it is teaching or surgery or selling movie tickets, is bringing all your tools and heart to the task. Maybe your job and your clients or your boss aren't always the best, but you have to be the best, because that's who you are.

And in the mists of time, a shirtless boy, the spring sun dappling his back, hoists an axe and a chainsaw and walks into the log yard.

Nursing is Cool and Nursing is Hot

Health careers are certainly hot commodities currently, with all of us boomers starting to creak audibly, and the population in general determined to consume every gram of fat attached to a deep-fried Coronary Burger Combo, piggy-sized. No career is hotter than nursing, with demand for nurses showing no sign of cooling. When I was at the University of Portland Nursing School orientation with my daughter Sally years ago, some poor dad asked the dean "What is your job placement rate?" and everyone looked at him like he had just nominated Brittany Spears for Mother of the Year.

Our family has recently evaluated nursing as a career option. Many workers in many fields struggle with the meaning of their efforts. You read about these billionaire hedge fund managers heading off to Africa to dig wells in an attempt to add some other-directed legitimacy to their lives. Nurses don't have that problem. Their work is important, immediately meaningful, and in critical demand. When you, your kid, or your mom is sick, you want a good nurse even more than you want your X-Box 360 to boot properly.

Nursing in intellectually challenging. The fusion of biology, chemistry, pharmacology, anatomy, and all the nuances of interpersonal relations engage a person on many levels. Nurses make hundreds of judgments a day—assessing patients, calculating and delivering medications, and planning the care of a patient in their recovery. They also have the challenge of dealing with certain powerfully charismatic, magnetic plastic surgeons who, when finally appreciated, will have their own TV shows.

Nursing is diverse. This last summer, my daughter met a nurse who is the CEO of a hospital chain in California. A former Chief Operating Officer at St. Vincent Healthcare in Billings was a nurse. Billings Clinic has had fine nurse executives. Hillary Clinton is a nurse (just kidding—no nurse I know would have allowed Bill to remain living). Nurses work everywhere from pediatric ICUs to the OR to the cath lab to specialty clinics. Nurses fly in helicopters and see acute situations in the ER. We have three nurses in our plastic surgery practice, and they do a tremendous variety of tasks—from assisting in surgery, patient counseling, office procedures, spa skin care, and preoperative planning. Nurses often have many roles during their career, which allows them to adapt their schedules to changing life circumstances, seek a new intellectual challenge, or pursue a particular career track. Companies that sell medical devices and products frequently recruit nurses to fill lucrative positions. Want to work in a particular location? There isn't any place on the planet right now that doesn't need a nurse.

One misconception that is somewhat still prevalent, although less so in recent years, is that nursing is a women's career only. I have worked with a number of outstanding male nurses in my career, guys that have bailed me out on more than one occasion. I enjoy a good deal of mutual respect with these men. Just as having more female physicians has balanced medicine, I think more male nurses will help address the shortage, as well as provide a lot of men with satisfying careers.

It is never too soon to begin preparing for a nursing career. Nursing school is hard, frankly, and you had better come ready to play. High school students should take the most challenging biology, chemistry, and social science classes they can. College biology is no place for beginners, so get a solid high school experience. I would also encourage early experience in the health care field, such as taking a nurse assistant course so you can work as an aide. Nursing school admission is competitive, so don't screw around in high school or in the first year or so of college and expect to get admitted. Once you get into nursing school, however, there are many scholarship programs to help keep you there, offered by everyone from hospital chains to the military.

As our family went through the evaluation of nursing, we ultimately felt that the wide variety of experiences and career options made the investment in nursing school a good choice. My daughter had considered medical school, but looking at four years of college, four years of medical school, five years of residency, and probably around 300 grand in debt, she wasn't thrilled. In addition, she saw the more immediate patient contact in nursing to be more satisfying to her personally. She also mentioned "I am not as full of myself as you are, Dad." Now what could she possibly mean by that?

So You Want To Be A Doctor

My first job was selling lemonade on the University golf course in Missoula in about 1820. My brother and I sold rather dilute Countrytime at ten cents a cup, and made even more money selling new Titleists back to people who had just lost them. Then the high school cheerleaders found out about the gig, no doubt from our own incontinent hubris, and set up on the hole in front of us. Bikini clad and considerably less rapacious, they quickly eliminated our market position. Ruined and chastened, I found a job building log homes.

Popular culture is rife with tales of awakening—whether it is physical, spiritual, or intellectual—mine was more related to power tools. Chainsaws, chisels, axes, skill saws, and drills all connected me to the deep collective subconscious of the craftsperson. I found I loved touching and cutting and molding and shaping and creating. Those of you who paint, sculpt, hang sheet rock, frame houses, plumb, wire, lay tile, bend sheet metal, sew, make jewelry, quilt—you all know what I mean. There is a certain sensual, ineffable joy in doing something with your hands. At the end of the day in the log yard, I would linger in the buttery summer light to savor the log home on which I had labored, and note what I did well and what I might do better.

So what does a nerdy kid with an aptitude for science and a proclivity for construction do? Surgery. My first operation was on a teddy bear named Cinnamon Bear, whose internal music box had quit working. I cut open the poor bear and sewed him back up. My mildly alarmed parents asked the pediatrician about this sort of behavior, and he helpfully told them that there really isn't much difference between a psychopath and a surgeon; you just need to keep them on the right track.

One of the first trauma cases I did as a surgical resident was a stab wound to the heart. We had quickly opened the chest as the guy was about dead, and there was a hole in the right ventricle spurting blood. I started to reach for a stitch or a clamp or anything, but the bemused and utterly calm professor said "just put your finger on the hole." And it worked. We got control of the situation; got him fluid resuscitated, and then leisurely sewed up the hole. I had my finger on a hole in this furiously thrashing heart, and I thought "this is cool like the log yard, only edgier."

During surgery one palpates the liver or lungs for tumors, uses a finger to peel an inflamed appendix from the abdominal wall, squeezes gallstones from the bile duct, or pulls organs up from the depths for examination. The hands and the brain are in constant dialogue—is this a tumor or inflammation? How big is this mass? Do I have room to sew this back together? Can I get a stapler in there? In plastic surgery we are constantly stretching, trimming, shaping, and molding until things look and feel right. It is an intensely tactile world.

One of the unfortunate ironies of medicine is that there are some brilliant people who desperately want to be surgeons, but weren't graced with the necessary physical coordination. I remember one such unfortunate soul who was struggling through a routine operation during his training. The supervising professor said "Marty, watching you operate is like watching geriatric pornography." Marty went happily into research. There are also surgeons with incredible physical skills that are weeded out because they lack good judgment or are medical airheads. I worked with a brilliant pediatric heart surgeon who had the personality of a great white shark, but had the sense to hire warm fuzzy people to talk to the patients. Then there are the rare surgical geniuses that have it all, who just happen to like Montana, and certain creative surgical disciplines, and have a background in lemonade sales.

While it is essential to have a fine touch, coordination, and a discerning fingertip, the most essential use of a health care provider's hand is another kind of touch. We are becoming a more latex-gloved, plastic-wrapped, gated-up, insular people. Whether you are a nurse, a doctor, an aide, a friend, or a parent, often an ill person needs an affirming hand on a shoulder or a trembling hand stilled. In illness, so much is intellectually opaque but viscerally known, and fear retreats before a confident hand. A hand that says, "you are not alone, I am with you" reaches a reservoir of healing that no drug or scalpel can.

To complete my career cycle, I just need to convince the OR supervisors to sterilize my power tools.

Chapter 4
Medicine And The
Rest of the World

The interface of medicine and society involves everything from how we handle booze to how we age, and what we do when life changes unexpectedly.

〜〜〜〜〜〜〜〜〜〜〜〜

Am I Too Old To Die?

How old would you be if you didn't know how old you were?—Satchel Paige

Groucho Marx said that age was not a very interesting subject. "Anyone can get old, all you have to do is live long enough."

The issue of age comes up a lot for surgeons. Every presentation about a patient begins with "This is a sixty-four year old...." Age is always first. A person's age is a significant "profiler," that is it speaks volumes about what might or might not be going on with a patient. A ten year old is not going to have coronary artery disease, Alzheimer's disease, or likely to have a stroke. We make a lot of assumptions based on age.

So what role does age play in terms of making decisions about surgery? When is someone too old for an operation?

I believe there is a great deal of age prejudice in our society. Certainly Madison Avenue lavishes advertising dollars on youthful images. I see ads in men's magazines for four hundred dollar shirts and six thousand dollar suits, and the models look like twenty year old sexually ambiguous smack addicts, and I wonder where they would have gotten the money for clothes that middle-aged plastic surgeons are too cheap to buy. Or maybe Madison Avenue doesn't see the point in marketing to cheap middle-aged plastic surgeons. But I digress.

Apart from a youth obsessed culture, older patients may face a certain degree of patronizing behavior from their children and physicians. I have seen children browbeat their parents into big operations they don't really want, because the kids have this fantasy that mommy and daddy will live forever if only they get that heart valve replaced. Physicians may not consider certain procedures because of the age listed on the chart. Often older patients are not listened to carefully because they are older, and are judged too feeble to fend for themselves. It may be they are judged so because they don't agree with their children or the doctor.

Here's how I handle the age business. First of all, no matter what your age, you really need to have your wits about you. I have found that even early dementia can be a problem with larger operations. If you or a loved one is a couple of tacos short of a combo, things might get very stressful after surgery. Back in my cardiac surgery days, I found that major heart or lung operations often pushed marginal individuals from independent living to nursing home. The argument would be made "Well, without this operation he/she might die!". Well, sometimes there are things worse than death, such as being stuck rotting in the ICU. On the other hand, if a person is sharp, I don't deny them what they want because of a number. If they are 85 with a good heart, clear lungs, and an OK from their internist, yeah, I will do a facelift on them if they really want it. But I do believe mental status is critical.

Then there are the basics. A history of heart attack, angina, or other coronary artery disease risk factors, including age, has to be evaluated. I worry a lot more about these factors than I do chronological age. If there is doubt, some type of provocative stress testing is appropriate, whether it is breast reconstruction, hip surgery, or my latest Brazilian Tush Tuck. Most non-smoking eighty-year-olds do better with surgery than a sixty-year-old smoker, both in terms of healing and lung complications. Control of diabetes also has a big impact on the outcome of surgery, regardless of age.

40

One factor that I think is underestimated in terms of age and surgical risk is social support. Having a supportive spouse, even a fairly useless one, improves outcome after surgery. (It amazes me how helpless some men get as they age, and how their wives let them do it.) Having children around (as long as they don't hijack the agenda) is obviously helpful. What really bugs me is when the yuppie kids fly in from Denver and Seattle, give me lots of orders, and then bolt on the second postoperative day when the real work begins. (That wasn't a digression, that was a rant. Different.) Having concerned people around, especially during recovery, really improves results in older people.

Bottom line—don't do anything you don't really want to do. If you don't, in your heart, want to go through something, even if it is life or death, don't do it. Your life, your call. If you are facing a big operation, and there are doubts about your fitness, get your internist or family physician involved to see if you can survive an assault from a knife-happy surgeon like me or one of my home boys (or girls).

Don't get hung up on the age number. Do concentrate on mental status, cardiovascular fitness, medical issues, and social support. Again, Satchel Paige: "Age is a case of mind over matter. If you don't mind, it don't matter."

Road Trip or Road Kill?

Trauma care is a significant part of plastic surgery practice. We're involved with everything from facial fractures to disfiguring cuts to repairing holes anywhere in the body.

As a result, I have had a good deal of exposure to patients who have been in car and motorcycle crashes. Part of the history I take from the patient is the cause and nature of the crash.

Over the years, I have learned that there are a few consistent themes behind most crashes.

• Driver inexperience: In my surgical training, I'll bet I helped on more than 1,000 surgical cases before I got to do one myself.

The professor would tell me, "This is someone's life; we can't take a chance on a rookie mistake."

Isn't it ironic that we give the keys to a 4,000-pound machine to a 15-year-old with a few driver's ed courses? The death rate for 15- and 16-year-old drivers is twice that of even 18-year-olds. I see kids with permanent paralysis, disfigured faces or brain injuries who just weren't skilled or mature enough to be driving. So take a lesson from the surgical professors - graduated responsibility. Give them lots of experience, but with you in the car. Start talking to your child at an early age about the decisions you make driving, what to watch out for, when to anticipate the idiot in the other lane making a stupid pass. Would you let a medical student with six weeks of training take out your appendix? Of course not. So don't turn a child loose in a life or death situation in a car. I don't care what the laws are, most kids don't have the experience they need.

• Driver fatigue: Recently I repaired the ravaged face of a nice lady who fell asleep trying to push a cross-country drive at 5 in the morning. I think I did a nice job on her face, but I can't fix a huge scar she will always have. Her 10-year-old boy was crushed when the car rolled, and he was dead at the scene.

The majority of Montana fatalities are single-car crashes, many of which are caused by people falling asleep. Don't drive when you ordinarily aren't awake. If you go to bed at 11 p.m. usually, then don't drive after that. Biorhythms are real things, so don't go against them. How many college kids have we seen killed trying an all-nighter from Portland or Seattle to Billings trying to get home for break? Don't let your kids do that - get them a plane ticket or a motel room. The second you feel tired driving, stop. Killing a loved one or sitting in a chair for the rest of your life isn't worth a small time savings.

• Driver restraints: Getting thrown out of a car at 80 mph isn't good. Duh. Three-quarters of fatalities are unrestrained passengers or drivers. Your face looks like a pizza when it hits the windshield. Being fed through a tube in your stomach while you gaze stupidly out the window of your nursing home is crazy fun. Just put on the seat belt, and insist that everyone in the vehicle wear one. And while you are at it, slow down.

• Bad timing: Stay home after midnight. Most Division I drunks don't get rolling until then. Stay out of their way. Watch the paper and see how many car crashes occur in the early morning hours. Animals are harder to see at night also. Ask any trauma surgeon about driving after midnight - they are the ones who have to come in and clean up the mess.

• Alcohol: What more can be said about this? Montana is one of the nation's leaders in drunken driving. One beer may not make you legally impaired but it might put you to sleep. Make your wife drive, that's what I do. She gets the moral high ground and it saves you her booze money.

Instead of quibbling with an officer about how many drinks you had, just have a sober driver. Teach your kid to be the designated driver.

I can't tell you how bad the emergency room smells on a Friday night from all the vomiting, smashed-up drunks, and how much screaming and whining these tough guys do when the orthopedist straightens out their pretzeled-up leg. Booze and cars - it ain't pretty.

It is completely ridiculous how many people die or are maimed in this state in cars. Can you imagine the uproar if 300 people died from West Nile virus, or food poisoning, or a serial killer? Drivers have to stop this. Our highway patrol officers are working hard, and these people are, in my experience, fine professionals who are very compassionate.

We have to stop this slaughter, especially of kids. So teach your children well. Show them, for years, how to be a good driver. If you catch your kid unrestrained or drinking, yank the car for six months. Don't drive late at night or early in the morning if you aren't ordinarily awake.

I know, a sober, belted, attentive (not even on a cell phone!) and slow driver is the antithesis of the iconoclastic Montana free spirit.

But maybe it's time to leave the roadkill to the skunks.

Bail Yourself Out Of Trouble

I had this horrible dream the other night. I was in the hospital, doing a completely unnecessary operation. I operated on the wrong side, completely botched the procedure, caused a lot of bleeding, and bumped off the patient. I staggered out of the hospital into a cacophonous thunderstorm, and a dark apparition appeared, thrusting a briefcase in my hand. Bewildered, I opened it, and there was 18 million dollars in cash. I woke up in a drenching sweat and related the dream to my wife. "Honey, you can relax, you are NOT a Wall Street investment banker."

So you have an upcoming operation, say hip replacement, hysterectomy, prostatectomy, or hopefully, an extensive cosmetic procedure. What should you be doing as a patient to achieve the best possible outcome?

Principle number one is to be a pest. Make sure you understand exactly what the procedure is, where it is, and what the alternatives are. Ask to see diagrams, have the surgeon draw the incision on your body, and look at models together if appropriate. Taking the mystery out of surgical procedures also helps to reduce the anxiety. This stuff ain't rocket science, frankly, and if the surgeon can't explain it fairly simply, find one who can. I am a big believer in rapport. If you feel uncomfortable with the surgeon, or don't like them, or they seem in a rush or distracted, keep shopping. There is no shortage of personable, skilled surgeons around here, especially, shall we say, mature plastic surgeons that really ought to have their own TV shows.

Ask frankly about alternatives. Don't be afraid about annoying the surgeon, and don't be intimidated. The day of the God Doctor is over. You are the consumer; they are the provider, so make them earn their money. Ask about non-surgical alternatives, and ask the surgeon to compare the results of surgical versus non-surgical therapies. Am I more likely to be alive in ten years if I have coronary bypass or if I take medication? Should I have medicine, radiation, or surgery for my prostate cancer? How many patients after back surgery still have pain a year after surgery? How soon can you do my breast implants? (Product warning: gratuitous drop-in sentence). You never HAVE to have an operation, so don't let anyone tell you that. Sometimes surgery is by far the best choice, but there are a lot of gray areas.

Get in shape for your operation. Studies have show that a month of preoperative exercise will improve postoperative outcome. You should run at least five miles a day prior to a hip replacement. Well, maybe that is not a good example. Who are you to question me, I'm a doctor. Anyway, it really works. If you can't walk, get in the pool and walk. Get a good month of workouts in and you will have fewer problems and recover more quickly.

I know everyone is totally saturated with the yap, yap, yap about smoking, but dude, just this once, check it out. Smoking just trashes the healing process. Spine surgeons watch their bone fusions melt away, and bone healing in general is severely impaired because nicotine and carbon monoxide squeeze off the tiny blood vessels that lead to healing. As plastic surgeons, we can't do facelifts, breast reductions, breast lifts, tummy tucks, or immediate breast reconstructions on smokers because the effect on skin flaps is so devastating. Smokers obviously have a lot more postoperative pneumonias and blood clots as well. Two months of cessation is preferable, but any time off is better than none.

A few quickies—if you have a history of urinary tract infections, get your urine checked a week before surgery so you don't get cancelled out for that. Ask your surgeon about how they feel about aspirin, drugs like ibuprofen, or any other blood thinner. Use an antibacterial soap the night before surgery. Ask about your prescriptions before surgery to clear up any allergy or intolerance issues. If you get stuck with some brutally expensive drug, it is not illegal to call from the pharmacy and ask the doctor's office to substitute a generic. Ask about any dressing supplies that might be necessary postop and get them in.

Many surgeons have nurses in the office who can be very helpful with postoperative questions. Try to identify that contact before surgery. While your surgeon might be very skilled, they may be clueless about your poorly fitting dressing bra, and besides, they're probably surfing the Internet looking for adult sized jammies with the attached feet.

Plan out your situation for once you are home. Will you need help? Will you need transitional care or a temporary nursing home? Is your spouse about as helpful as a cold sore? Get this figured out before your brain is full of Percocet. It is more useful for your grown son or daughter to come not for the surgery, but for the home care.

Discuss the financial arrangements with the doctor's office and the insurance company so you don't get hit with a big surprise. Don't dilly-dally on the preauthorization stuff. Take the stress off yourself by being prepared. Check the office tipping policy. This improves your chances of being on the TV show.

The longer I practice (insert boring aphorism here) the more I believe in instincts. If you feel good about the procedure, it has been well explained, and it makes sense to you in your metaphysical gut, go for it. Conversely, if you're not feeling good about something, it doesn't feel right, then don't do it. It is always your life, your body, and your choice. A good surgeon has no problem seeing you for an extra visit in the office, or calling your deadbeat son-in-law in California who watches a lot of medical shows.

Being a patient has become much less of a passive and more of a participative process. The success of your procedure has a lot to do with your planning and preparation. Somehow I don't think any of that 700 billion dollar bailout has your name on it.

How About A Gossip Column?

In between surgical cases I'll head to the staff lounge to do a little chilling, make some calls, and maybe have a snack. Every lounge has a TV, and it seems inevitably that someone has turned to one of the "news" channels. It used to be the stock market channel, but even the most mercenary among us has decided that financial news is too depressing. What passes for "news" now is televised tabloid. Congressman caught in a New Orleans hotel dressed up in a Little Bo Peep costume, accompanied by an ounce of cocaine and a 21 year old intern in a cheerleader's outfit. Stoic wife, standing bravely in front of the camera saying, "Let's not jump to conclusions." Right. My wife would not jump to conclusions either. She'd jump to a pair of industrial-grade bolt cutters.

Another story: a news organization actually reporting on the goings-on of a reality television show—Mr. and Mrs. No Life prepping their six urchins for a lifetime of state-sponsored psychotherapy. All this "news" is delivered by exquisitely prepped young female models, I mean journalists. It seems all "news" now is geared for our brainstem, if not lower.

All except the Health Section. Here you get carefully thought out, sober, educational, and well-meaning information and advice from experienced professionals, who, with the exception of the brooding, masculine, charisma-oozing threat that is the plastic surgery writer, are pretty much Centrum Silver models rather than CNN anchors. I am beginning to see this approach as a problem.

How many articles have we all written about good nutrition, smoking cessation, exercise, wearing seatbelts, getting colonoscopy and mammography, watching your blood pressure, blah, blah, blah? After all that effort and ink, obesity continues to rise. The average American in the last fifteen years has gone from a cornerback to an offensive lineman. Smoking rates actually *increased* last year. Reluctantly, I have come to the conclusion that we had better get with it. Real news isn't working.

I'm thinking about chucking the whole information/education thing and going with a medical gossip column. After all, health care is one of the major economic engines in this area, and yet we have little if any "news", that is dirt, about this important subject.

So let's see, let's try out a few ideas. What well-known cardiologist was seen canoodling in a cozy corner of Enzo's last week with a shapely someone? Hmm...has potential, but there are a few problems. First, they're married, they're more than a five iron from young, and by shapely, it might be a bit more Barbara Bush than Barbie. They're killing time waiting to pick their kid up from play practice, and since it's nearly eight o'clock, they are exchanging yawns like a Federer-Nadal rally. No wine either—it gives them both reflux.

Ok, how about this: What prominent orthopedic surgeon bombed out of his junior high spelling bee because he couldn't spell the word "kat"? They even spotted him the "k" and the "t", and he still couldn't get it write. It's a good piece of dirt, but all the parents of the budding athletic superstars care is that he can spell ACL.

What internist cum U-12 girls soccer coach ran his girls through three hour practices in subfreezing weather this last fall? No, that won't work. The majority of soccer coaches would consider that soft, quitting at three hours when you don't have to worry about heat exhaustion.

What local medical power players have had facelifts, botox, liposuction, etc? Answer: None of them. They're too cheap. That I know for sure. Their idea of a cosmetic procedure is to use a toothpick before seeing office patients.

I don't know, it's not looking too promising. Frankly, there's not a lot to work with here. Maybe we'll have to play it straight here in the health section.

So much of health relates to how much respect we have for our minds and bodies. I know how agitated I get when my kids lose or drop or damage their cell phones, ipods, bikes, coats, etc. Like every parent I rail, "You have no respect for the effort it takes…" you know that sermon. We'll fawn over a prize possession such as a car or boat or motorcycle, and then allow our bodies to get soft and fat and sodden with booze, smoke, and dietary sludge. Poor God, who hands us this truly miraculous machine that is the human body, and we proceed to trash it. No wonder we have thunderstorms.

I think we are much more fastidious about what we put in our mouths than what we allow in our minds. Our attitudes and beliefs, our entire consciousness is subtly sculpted by what enters our eyes and ears. A computer aphorism states "garbage in, garbage out." Once we realize, sometimes through tragedy or a life altering experience, what a truly precious gift a human body and a human mind is, then we can really understand what stewardship of that gift means. So when I enter that lounge, and see that tawdry intellectual pollution that is the "news", I take a courageous step and turn the channel to ESPN.

What local plastic surgeon, at a recent benefit, inadvertently flexed his massive bronzed pec and tore an 800-dollar Italian linen shirt? Too obvious.

Changing Places: Flipping Out In Middle Age

No matter how young your girlfriend, or big your Harley, my mid-life crisis can top yours. I left a stable and respectable job as a heart surgeon and went back to school with a bunch of twenty-five year olds to become a plastic surgeon. I dragged a wife and three kids 1800 miles to the deep South, to Jackson, Mississippi, to new schools, in a strange land, at less than minimum wage. Why?

I came to Billings in 1991, and for 12 years was part of highly rated cardiovascular programs at the two excellent hospitals we are privileged to have in this town. In those years I did around 1800 heart surgeries and as many vascular and thoracic surgery cases. But as many people in many jobs have experienced, technologies and markets change. The rise of catheter-based technologies such as balloons and stents to treat coronary blockages greatly reduced the number of heart surgeries. I also felt that having done many of the same operations over and over again, it would be fun as well as challenging to do something different.

Over the last few years, I had been talking with one of my intramural basketball buddies, Dr. Walter Peet, a plastic surgeon, about what he did. He spoke of the great diversity in the field— everything from the repair of complex congenital defects to trauma to aesthetic surgery. He also mentioned that he was retiring in 2005, and leaving behind a good young partner in Dr. Steve Grosso. Billings would need another plastic surgeon, and it sure looked to me like it needed one less heart surgeon.

I was very fortunate to find a spot in a plastic surgery training program, as you can imagine it is a very hot field. It was quite an experience being a trainee again at the age of 46. My fellow trainees were 25-30 years old and played X-Box instead of watching the stock market channel. It was fun mentoring the surgery residents and teaching medical students. The faculty was about my age, and frankly, I think I made them nervous, as they weren't sure how to boss a board certified heart surgeon. I thoroughly enjoyed the cornucopia that is a plastic surgery residency—the tremendous variety of people and problems and procedures.

Living in the South was a great experience for me and my family. The gracious civility of the people, the manners, the food, the football—it was all rich and rewarding. We gained a new perspective on social and racial issues. We came to appreciate the strength and depth of the churches there. Pam, my wife, and my children Sally, Cathy, and Luke even sort of liked the heat and humidity.

The two years in training passed very quickly, and my practice here has been everything I could have hoped for. For the first time in my practice career, I have had a chance to work with kids. No two cases have been the same.

What did I learn? Circumstances change in your life and career, and what once was a very comfortable situation can become unstable. Even at 46, a person can make a big change. If you feel you have reached a professional plateau of sorts, you will probably serve yourself and your profession better if you invest in new skills and develop a new thematic string in your life.

Going back into training was an exercise in profound humility. Instead of being captain of the ship, I was bailing bilge water. I learned that people treat you based on how you carry yourself and the personal dignity you project, rather than your given title. I learned that someone who really loves you doesn't care if you go from somebody to nobody. Oh, and my family taught me one other lesson: "you can do this once, dude, and that's it!"

Chapter 5
I Need A New Drug

From motion sickness to narcotic bliss, from medical cannabis to big muscles, we're a drug crazed society.

~~~~~~

A Layman's Guide To Performance Enhancing Drugs

I want a new drug
One that won't make me sick
One that won't make me crash my car
Or make me feel three feet thick

--Huey Lewis and the News

I get very annoyed when I see Congress wasting time on things like climate change, a spiraling deficit, a couple of wars, and other trivial stuff. So when they recently had hearings to determine if a lump in baseball pitcher Roger Clemens buttock was, in fact, due to an injection of anabolic steroids, my faith in democracy was restored. One can just imagine a geek like Rep. Henry Waxman being shoved in a high school locker by someone like Roger Clemens, and Waxman's giddy pleasure in firing little bow-tied fast balls at Clemens head. Performance enhancing drugs are all the media rage today, from the Tour De France to track athletes to the NFL and Major League Baseball. It seems like everyone is juicing.

So what exactly are these drugs and why are they such a big deal? Are you behind the times, and should *you* be juicing? Has the guy in cubicle down your row got a chemical advantage that you've missed out on?

First of all, let no one get too pious about this subject. We all use performance-enhancing drugs. Coffee, for instance, is a powerful phosphodiesterase inhibitor, which translated means it relaxes smooth muscle, sharpens concentration and memory, and you know what all coffee does. Does a couple of pops of Chardonnay or gin decrease your social anxiety at an event? Do a few Motrin make that jog or racquetball game go a little smoother? Does a little Prozac or Paxil or Effexor or Xanax keep you from killing your spouse or kid? Let those without sin cast the first stone.

The two main players in the performance enhancement arena are steroids and human growth hormone. A steroid is a chemical compound composed of the sterol ring, which is three six carbon rings and one five-carbon ring. The molecule looks like chicken wire. The basic form is cholesterol, and all steroids are derived from this framework. There are many steroids naturally occurring in the body, and they are good and amazing molecules that regulate thousands of bodily functions. Most steroids have nothing to do with making big muscles. Testosterone is a steroid that does make big muscles, and this hormone has been a focus of intense study.

Testosterone is the principle hormone in humans that produces male secondary sex characteristics (androgenic), and is an important hormone in tissue healing and maintenance of muscle mass (anabolic). Scientists have fiddled around with the testosterone molecule to try to augment one effect or another. For instance, the East German female shot putters in the old days had to shave twice a day, so scientists worked to reduce the androgenic effects (making you more of a guy) and increase the anabolic effects (make your muscles bigger). So by adding various other carbons and oxygens and such to the steroid rings, scientists were able to make testosterone derivatives that were more specifically anabolic (build you up) and less androgenic (mellow on the wolf man.) These derivatives have cool names like Danazol, Stanazol, and Anadrol-50.

Testosterone derivatives act inside the cell on specific testosterone receptors, which in turn give instructions to the RNA in the cells to pump you up. These compounds have been widely used by athletes the world over to increase strength, hasten healing, and to tremendously accelerate the training process.

So, you young aspiring local stud athlete, why not juice? Well, your acne explodes, your hair falls out, you develop psychotic rage with the slightest provocation, your eyes turn yellow, you start growing female appearing breasts, and yes, your package shrinks. I don't care if you become a four-year starter; none of the above is okay. Forget the long-term consequences of malignant tumors and sterility, when things start to shrivel up...

What about human growth hormone (HGH)? It works very well for children with short stature and measurable growth hormone deficiency. Adult growth hormone deficiency is a very controversial area, and some semi-shady physicians have made an industry out of finding growth hormone deficiency in adults and then treating it with injections. Most studies have found that using human growth hormone in the absence of a major deficiency really doesn't help performance.

If you really want to improve performance, genetics is the way to go. Young people really need to consider this carefully. For instance, my wife is attractive, bright, supportive, loving, blah, blah, blah. But she has no hops, can't dribble to the left at all, and has no jump shot beyond 15 feet. Should I have pursued that girl in high school whose sister is in the WNBA? No one tells you this stuff when you are young and suffused with lust. Years later, when your kid clanks one shot after another, it comes home to roost. And these families around town that crank out one star quarterback and point guard after another? Those kids are all coming from a secret, exclusive embryo bank in Switzerland. Don't tell anyone.

Performance enhancing drugs are the ultimate Faustian bargain—a chance to achieve a dream at the cost of health and reputation. Do you think Barry Bonds is a happy guy? Is a piece of Floyd Landis' soul lying somewhere on a road in the

Alps? Is the most significant line in sports no longer the goal line but the line between clean and dirty? These are important conversations to have at the dinner table. Now if we can just get Congress interested in the real world....

The Walking Wasted

Our current shoebox office is essentially a hallway with a few small rooms and a niche that functions as a kitchen. Anywhere I move in the office I go by the "kitchen". We are fortunate to have many skilled bakers as patients, and also patients with whom we have hung in with through long sieges of wounds or illnesses who express their gratitude with creations from one of our many wonderful local bakeries.

I consider myself a reasonably sober, temperate individual with a moderate degree of impulse control, but I have an extremely difficult time walking by a warm, soft, cinnamon raisin roll and not covertly ripping a chunk out of it.   Since I pass by that area approximately 192 times during an office day, the caloric implications are catastrophic.

Our new facility will have an actual kitchen and break room, but it will be roughly a half a mile from my office, which my staff and the architect placed behind the dumpster outside. The ramifications are clear—a high caloric munchie will require volition beyond impulse—a walk of shame through the reception area and past the censorious eyes of team members who feel I should be addressing the mountain of charts on my desk instead of carbo-loading.

It may be that those without sin are simply those without the opportunity to sin.

The issue of drug abuse in the health care professions is seemingly eternal. As a child I used to hang out with my mother pharmacist at the hospital, and I vividly remember a physician dropping by on a Friday afternoon to pick up a few Demerol tablets for a weekend trip with the boys. An old friend of mine became addicted to cough syrup samples with hydrocodone.

54

Recently in town here we have seen high profile cocaine busts involving health care providers, and at least yearly there are physicians caught writing narcotics prescriptions for themselves. One popular strategy is to cultivate an insalubrious patient with a cocaine or meth connection, then trade Percocet prescriptions for the blow.

Like everyone else, doctors and other providers have problems with our Hall of Fame drug, alcohol. As a surgical resident, I had the ultimate in back handed compliments from one of my supervising faculty—"I feel comfortable getting sloshed when you are on call, because I know you can do the operation fine without me." Swell.

Why do doctors and other health care workers get mixed up in drug abuse? I do think availability has a lot to do with it. Anesthesia, with its plethora of chemical goodies, is especially risky. Although there are strict rules of accounting for narcotics, nurses and doctors and pharmacists aren't stupid people, and there are always ways of beating it.

Honestly, I think there are doctors who are smart, nerdy types who could get into medical school, cleaned up on tests, and mastered resume building-- but haven't got the mental toughness for the job. You have to be able to handle pressure, make decisions with the bullets flying, and be able to pick yourself up after getting beaten or humiliated. I have made my share of bad decisions, I have hurt people, and I have baggage that I will always sadly bear. What I do have is excellent training, enough ego to survive, and most of all a support system of friends, family, my partner, and my staff. Many providers don't have that, and loneliness combined with a feeling of fraud and inadequacy is a short trip to the Cocaine Café. There are a very few practitioners who use because they just like getting high, but a great majority who live in a miserable miasma of dread.

There is an extremely rigorous monitoring program for providers who are found to be using, whether it is narcotics or problem alcohol. Rehab is not optional if you want to get a license back, and drug tests and monitoring after rehab are extensive. The medical profession is accused at times of protecting its own and covering up things, which I think in some cases is true, but not with substance abuse.

Solutions? At times I think this whole society is walking around wasted. There are way too many narcotics being handed out, because patients demand them and doctors want to shut them up. Most studies show that ibuprofen is as effective as oxycodone or hydrocodone for pain relief, but ibuprofen doesn't give you that warm fuzzy cloud to sit on. After that knee scope by Dr. Knuckledragger, use the strong meds for a day or two, then throw them away before you start cloud sitting (or your medicine cabinet trolling teenager does.)

One surgery professor told me "Don't ever think you are better than you are—drugs, cheating, money, booze—whatever. You're just another animal dressed up in a white coat. It'll keep you out of trouble."

To my faithful reading patients, do not, repeat, do not quit bringing the cinnamon rolls, frosted, with raisins, whole wheat is especially fine. I will never learn to develop a stronger character and face those demons of impulsivity by the destructive process of denial. The walk to the kitchen will be good exercise.

Mary Jane and Medicine

My Wednesday office days are usually highly social occasions—seeing old patients, now friends, with whom I have been through long battles of cancer reconstruction, wound closures, burns, car wrecks, or congenital deformities. I meet new patients, and whether we are discussing face-lifts or skin cancers, I am struck by how similar our desires and dreams and problems are as muddling mortals. I wasn't prepared, though, when a patient asked me if her lingering back and shoulder pain from an old injury might benefit from medical marijuana.

I am not at all qualified to discuss marijuana. One of the disadvantages of leading a spotless, blameless, virtuous life is a lack of knowledge regarding the seamy underbelly of society.

I have never touched a drop of alcohol. There are certainly no pictures of me in an orange jumpsuit with the printed words "Gallatin County", following a college incident in a bar involving a misdirected pitcher of beer, for instance. Those sorts of allegations are part of a vast ambidextrous conspiracy. And I most certainly did not have a business in college "polishing" term papers for a dollar and a beer per page, some of the pages being devoid of ink entirely and thus requiring a great deal of polishing, two beers a page if you wanted an A. That would have been wrong.

So lacking any knowledge of vice in general, I researched the issue of medical marijuana and found, well, not much. There is certainly a great deal of political and emotional rhetoric, but as a clinician I have no use for that. I need data, randomized controlled trials, nerdy stuff.

The Drug Enforcement Agency (DEA) regulates drugs on a schedule, and marijuana is currently listed as schedule I, meaning it has no proven benefit and is considered dangerous. Heroin is a schedule I drug. It is also classified as an illicit drug by the federal government. Those carefully controlled studies I would like to see are difficult to do on a schedule I illegal drug, because you aren't supposed to have it. The primary active ingredient in marijuana is THC, which is available and on the market as a pill (Marinol), but most scientists and stoners alike agree that marijuana is much more potent when smoked.

Marijuana leaves (I am told) vary vastly in potency from exotic Hawaiian buds to the lawn clippings the guy down the hall in the dorm sold, rather, might sell to someone in a hypothetical dorm, somewhere. There is simply no way to measure the potency of and thus the efficacy of a substance when you have no idea what the concentration is, and then no idea what the delivery and absorption rates are. All you can observe is the effect, which makes us medical numbers geeks very nervous.

And how do I order it? Two tokes every four hours as needed? One ounce Mexican Red Hair, one refill? Does it come generic?

The American Medical Association and the American Cancer Society have not endorsed the use of marijuana, but have rather stated that while there is not solid clinical evidence for its use, patients certainly have the right to make their own choices.

Marijuana has most been used medically for nausea in HIV and cancer patients, to stimulate appetite (if you see six guys buying three dozen rolls and a gallon of raspberry jam at Safeway at two in the morning you probably don't need clinical studies on appetite) and for treatment of pain. The booming medical marijuana business in Montana (a recent full page ad in the Missoulian featured a "provider list") is primarily fueled by individuals with some sort of pain condition. Interestingly, marijuana possession is still considered a federal offense, but the Justice Department has elected not to prosecute individuals with a medical marijuana "certificate". However, you can be fired from your job if you test positive for marijuana. To say that medical marijuana is legally murky is, like, really, I forgot what I was talking about. Don't eat all the jam.

Chronic pain is an extremely difficult condition. There is no way to measure it. As a provider, how do you know if someone is really hurting or just wants drugs? In many cases, you don't. And when does the treatment reinforce the pain, i.e. "if I feel pain, then I can have the dope." And medically, we just don't have very good pain medicines. If they don't addict you, then they make you constipated or nauseated or break out in a rash. I've had the experience of family members with awful conditions like rheumatoid arthritis who never experienced any real relief. Pain treatment is an area of medicine that could really use a big breakthrough.

I don't doubt that "medical" marijuana is preemptory to legalization of the drug altogether. I am ambivalent about that as many of you are. I see the slaughter in Billings from all the alcohol road deaths, the relentless devastation of alcoholism in all tiers of our social stadium, and the icy grip that prescription narcotics is gaining over so many people. Ask any doctor; the number of people taking oxycontin or hydrocodone and other buzz bombs has skyrocketed. Frankly, I don't see that many stoners in the ER unless their tox screen is positive for ten other things.

My real concern as a physician is that marijuana be evaluated in the same way we evaluate all other drugs and therapies. Or, maybe, leave me out of it all together. I don't think medical doctors have all the answers. My bigger concern is that of a society whose spiritual and social content is being replaced by chemical content. Marijuana has a potent effect on the nervous system because we are built with cannibinoid receptors that go nuts when the bong hits the brain, just as we have opiate receptors that make nice little warm fluffy clouds when the Percocet kicks in. Taking a hit or popping a pill is a whole lot easier than exercising hard or building a relationship or accomplishing a goal, things that are hard fought but give us that natural endorphin rush that is ever so transient, but is the apogee of human existence. At times I envision a future with humans as soft, doughy creatures nestled home alone, antidepressed, narcotized, stoned; gazing dreamily at a video screen on which is depicted someone else's life. No chance for loss, no chance for gain, no real feeling at all. Where's that bag of rolls?

Summer Vacation Is A Recreational Drug

This is the time of year when I become excited about the end of school, summer break, and a return to my summer job of building log homes in the Swan Valley. At some point I remember that it has been thirty years since I last had a summer break, that I am a grown-up who will not be paroled in June, and that encroaching dementia is now more my companion than an axe or a chain saw.

The spring winds of social change have swirled in my domicile, where I searched for my son the other evening. He was supposed to be doing geometry (an organic alternative to waterboarding), but I found him instead in front of the TV with the characteristic slack-jawed and vacuous mien of the video gamer engaged in some extremely sociopathic slaughter. I mentioned a recent edict banning video games on school nights. "These aren't video games," he replied without missing a knife kill, "my legs are sore after track practice and I am treating them with medical X-Box. I got a green card."

Meetings respect no seasonal boundaries. Hospitals are governed by committees which look at things like patient safety, physician performance, specialty areas such as cancer or trauma, and which ridiculously expensive robot to buy to get ahead of brand X.

My most recent meeting was the Facial Trauma Call Group. Plastic surgeons, oral surgeons, and Ear, Nose, and Throat doctors share the responsibility for responding to Emergency Room calls for patients with facial trauma. Various calamities have reduced the number of doctors available for this call. There was really nothing to discuss (like most meetings, yours included), because the only solution was for everyone left standing to take more call. This onerous proposition poisoned the meeting from the start, with the general surliness and lethargy exacerbated by the 0630 start.

There are a limited number of ways to acquire facial trauma. A nice, well-meaning soul can catch an elbow to the nose in a game, a fitness nut tumbles off his 8500-dollar Trek, or a worker takes a two by six to the snoot. These, unfortunately, are the distinct minority. Our facial trauma customers fall into two general groups.

The first is a youngish male with an alcohol level of oh, about .256 (legally sloshed is .08), who has also smoked pot, snorted meth, snacked on some purloined Percocets, and swallowed a half dozen stool softeners from his grandma's medicine cabinet, thinking there were Valiums, the aforementioned substances having impaired his usually acute judgment regarding pharmaceuticals. He hops in his unregistered truck at about 0130 and proceeds down a windy two-lane road at 106 mph. He fails to negotiate a turn (the turn being rather inflexible in the negotiation) and the truck rolls 87 times, ejecting the driver (the failed negotiator, unencumbered by a seat belt), who then impacts a fence post with his face. By the time the patient's 16 other injuries are sorted through and the facial trauma guy is called, it is about 4:30 a.m.

The second group of facial trauma patients is similar. Take the same guy and put him in a bar, only a little drunker, say .345. He is still in the bar because he keeps trying to put his snowmobile key in his truck and has been thus unable to drive. He can, however, leer down the shirt of an attractive young woman, who is unfortunately attached to a considerably more sober, muscular, and jealous male companion. The companion's right fist impacts our patient's jaw, causing the mandibular ramus to split like dry kindling. These guys usually show up in the ER around noon on Sunday, prompted by a horrified one-eyed look in the mirror after regaining consciousness.

The exorbitant cost of recreational drugs precludes the purchase of health insurance, unfortunately, and so not only do these folks spit at you, try to bite you, and smell really bad from vomiting, they won't pay you and certainly can sue you. So, at 0630, at a meeting whose purpose is to increase the opportunity to care for these nice young men, the enthusiasm is low. The conscious participants ignore the audible snoring. When a vote is taken to rework the call schedule, the results are Aye 0, Nay 0, Whatever 8.

I grumble, we grumble. But what defines professionalism is that you get out of bed and do it. At 0430 you give that stinky, belligerent guy the best medical care on the planet, at times for free. One can argue that we have become a society without judgment or consequence, and that our pickled friend should lie in the field next to his truck and bleed. But that stupid kid might be my kid, who knows. So you get out of bed and just do it.

Forget medical marijuana. Forget medical X-Box. Get me a green card that says Summer Vacation.

Panty Hose As It Relates To Recreational Drugs

Those of you who have run cross-country or track, or who have children who have, or who have coached said sports are familiar with this phenomenon. The spring/fall weather will be close to idyllic all week, Montana in its seasonal glory. Then, Saturday morning, things begin to deteriorate, with a record setting snowstorm wrapped in a hurricane tortilla, usually peaking right about the start of the 800-meter run.

Such was the case at the state cross-country meet my senior year. All the way from Missoula to Helena the day before the race, the flurries built until it was necessary, the day of the race, to bring one of those big rotary plows down from MacDonald pass, to carve a tunnel on the golf course where the race was being held.

The blizzard did not abate, so between running through a gauntlet of ice and a wind composed of frigid razorblades, the circumstances were challenging for a wimp such as myself, whose mental toughness was already suspect.

In the mid 70s we wore those lumpy sweats, real sweats, in which we warmed up, stripping down at race time to wispy silks. The current crop of youth athletes, pampered and lavishly overindulged, will be wearing 500 bucks worth of UnderArmour/ Nike polypro/lycra if the temperature is less than 80. Not so in 1974. I did not wish to freeze to death. Friday afternoon I slipped away from the team and jogged to JC Penny.

The young woman there listened carefully to my plight. "Unless you want to totally tank the race", she advised, "You need something tight and flexible. Men don't wear that stuff. Let's go over to ladies petite."

The day of the race I waited as long as I could before removing the sweats. Unfortunately, not long enough. My coach, let us say, was not progressive. "What the @#$% are you wearing? Those look like pantyhose! You look like a (complex pejorative containing blasphemy/obscenity/suggestion that my anatomy was XX instead of XY. The kind of artfully constructed insult that only a 70s era experienced coach could conjure.)" He ordered me to remove them. I told him I would if he would remove the 14 layers of duck hunting gear he was wearing.

My archrival, a kid from Helena Capital, saw me and said, with blue lips "you look like a (adolescent permutation of the above, less nuanced)". He shivered involuntarily. "Penny's, about six blocks, ask for Helen, I recommend the black. You have time if you hurry," I said. He bolted. And later, he beat me.

62

I struggle with pain management. Medicine has tried and tried to come up with pain medicines that work for moderate to severe pain that aren't narcotics, but after a while they all get pulled off the market because they cause heart attacks or horns to grow on your forehead. We have the same pain meds, essentially, that we had 40 years ago. Maybe we should give the job to UnderArmour and Nike.

The way that Percocet and Lortab and Norco and Vicodin work is that they have some Tylenol in them for pain relief, and then some oxycodone or hydrocodone to relieve anxiety and mellow you out. Anxiety and fear are big components of the pain response. Multiple randomized, controlled studies have shown, that for pure pain relief, ibuprofen (Motrin, Advil) is as efficacious as narcotics. What narcotics do is create a warm, fuzzy cloud on which you can sit while your boo boo heals. The problem is, that warm fuzzy cloud can be a nice place even after your boo boo is gone.

One of my buddies in residency had no tolerance for drug seekers in the ER, of which there are many. The patients would come in with complaints of severe maladies and terrible pain, none of which could be proved, or unfortunately, disproved. He would tell them "look, pal, go home and take a handful of Motrin and wash it down with a couple of beers, like the rest of us."

Most of my patients, even after fairly big operations, take the narcotic pills for a couple of days and chuck them. Others want three refills. The guy who gets his jaw busted in a drunken fight will call daily for more drugs, whereas the guy who gets his jaw popped shoeing a horse will never call.

How many newspaper accounts have we read of the prescription drug abuse epidemic? I know very well that many prescriptions get sold, by the patient, their kids, or their "friends".

You see, my coach, in all his duck hunting gear, wouldn't feel my pain when I took off those sweats. He couldn't know. That's why this narcotic issue is hard for me, for all doctors.

Can we really know another? Think of that life partner, that soul mate, that love of a lifetime that dumped you without warning. A certain portion of our soul remains opaque, impenetrable, a room only one can enter. Often we don't know ourselves. Pain and illness are among the hardest human experiences to understand. Do we call in sick because we are going to a concert in Missoula, because we are barfing through our nose, or because we just can't emotionally step up to the plate today? (I think I am sorta getting the flu).

Human behavior is an undulating cauldron of emotions, experiences, cynical calculations, wants, needs, desires, and whatever else was in the cupboard when the creator was cooking. I know one thing for sure: I looked pretty good in panty hose.

Motion Sickness And Middle-Aged Wistfulness

The portrait of sublime contentment: An 18 month old boy sitting on the floor, surrounded by toy trucks and guns and action figures, his only garment a luxuriously padded extra absorbent diaper. That's why boys potty train later than girls— why drop your toys when there exists an already satisfactory management strategy? Boy's toys, assertive and active with a subtle palate of aggression, bring a sense of pleasure and control. Doing stuff is real, and it is good.

Dragons last forever, but not so little boys. We begin to become serious. We wonder if we are logical positivists or existentialists. We use words like "relationship." We seek education, certification, validation, enlightenment, advancement, and establishment of empire. I've even heard of men who, in their desire not to unduly burden the cleaning of the commode, sit down. Some join book clubs. They approve the purchase of a minivan.

It is hard to say when this weave of maturity, sobriety, and responsibility begins, ever so subtly, to unravel. Each tendril of adult rationalism thins, stretches, and rents, surrendering ever so incrementally, like an individual sunbeam at dusk. It is the achievement of the empire, the realization of goals, the forging of the golden calf that initiates the deconstruction of the midlife male. Sitting in the mahogany boardroom on the top floor, surveying his conquests literal or figurative, the conclusion for our Master of the Universe is clear: I'd rather be playing trucks.

The signs and symptoms, usually detected by wives and daughters first, with no small degree of alarm, are straightforward. Magazines and brochures relating to motorcycles, ATVs, guns of all sorts, non-functional cars, unwieldy trucks—fill in your own obsession/addiction here—you know who you are, or you are related to one—begin to accumulate. The subject speaks with an enthusiasm and animation not otherwise observed. There is pressured speech, dilated pupils, diaphoresis, and rather awkward analogies between double action shotguns and the eighth grade play.

How, you ask, does this pertain to motion sickness?

I have always liked boats, toy boats, aluminum boats, outboard motors, fiberglass boats.   My parents were supportive, because I had initially liked stuffed bears, but when I started operating on them they became alarmed. So now, 53 years of age, I want to drive a big boat. That means ocean, which means seasickness.

Motion sickness, a more general term for airsickness, carsickness, and seasickness is thought to result from the body's gyroscope, or vestibular system, disagreeing with the rest of the body. Unusual motions don't fit with our visual perceptions, and the brain thinks it is being poisoned, so the brain thinks we should throw up and get rid of the poison.

There are many suggested preventive strategies and remedies for motion sickness. Ginger root apparently works pretty well. It appears to relax the sphincter leaving the stomach. Pressure devices at the wrist in the form of a bracelet seem to work for some people.

Nausea and vomiting are mediated by the parasympathetic component of the autonomic nervous system, which controls our basic unconscious functions. A drug called scopolamine directly inhibits the end neurons of the parasympathetic system. For the last several years scopolamine patches, worn behind the ear, seem to have really helped with motion sickness. The problem with the patch has been dosage variation in terms of drug delivery and also the size of the patient.

Scopolomine has now been released in an oral form. It comes in 0.4 mg tablets. Our boating course a couple of weeks ago in Anacortes WA took place in a hurricane, so I gave one tablet to my son one hour before getting on a wildly rocking 40 foot trawler, two to my wife, and I took like ten of them. I'm lying. Again.

Bottom line, it worked very well. The side effects of dry mouth and slightly blurry vision were worth the fact that despite 6 to 8 foot seas and a wicked tide going the wrong way, we nearly died but did not get seasick. The wind was 35 knots, the rain was blowing sideways, and it never got above 40 degrees. It was awesome. My wife did say that she would be okay with a girlfriend, a Corvette, a hairpiece, and the biggest Harley on the lot if only we didn't have to do National Lampoon Perfect Storm Family Vacation again. It really didn't take me that long to turn around and get her after she got blown off.

Scopace, the oral scopolamine, is a prescription drug, so discuss it with your doctor, read the warnings, and whatnot.

How do we return to the garden of contentment? Do we explore eschatology to infer the will of the Divine? Or do we ponder the raw water-cooling system on a marine diesel engine? Do we explore semiotics to determine if language ultimately contaminates communication, or do we say the heck with it and spring for that new Winston fly rod?

It isn't a question of the intellectual versus anti-intellectual. What sustains us is the simple pleasure over the pretentious. Who needs kingdoms when you have a warm loving hand on your shoulder? Joy is only illusory or complicated when we misconstrue it. It may be on the floor next to us.

Chapter 6
MuskettCare

I could solve all the problems in health care with my plan, MuskettCare. Unfortunately, no one has asked me to solve anything. My plan involves a combination of the most politically unpopular positions ever, other than mandating government coverage of cosmetic surgery.

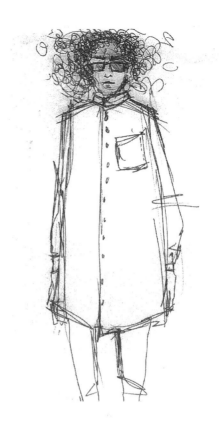

~~~~~~~~~~~~~~~~~~~~~~~~~~~~~~

Two Tiers

If there is one constant in these entertainingly chaotic political mud wrestling spectacles, it is the promise that we will have some sort of a national health care plan.

Health insurance costs are high, medical and prescription costs are usurious, and, as always, we Americans are entitled, by virtue of our ability to inhale and exhale, to the best of everything for free. Our senior Montana Senator, Mr. Baucus, has stated that Americans have a "God-given right to affordable health care." My knowledge of the Bible, the Torah and the Quran is pedestrian, I admit, but I do not recall a scriptural passage to that effect. I think Moses lost that tablet. Remember that God created Adam and Eve without clothes, but presumably with an affordable health plan, so where did they put their insurance card?

Anyway, it's going to happen, and I think I have a pretty good idea of what it is going to look like. I have worked in the Veterans Affairs system a fair bit during training, as well as a Public Health Hospital and some county hospitals. I suspect we will see a hybrid of these existing institutions.

Frequent mention is made of that fact that most Western industrialized countries have national health services, and that they are great, and everyone loves them, and so why don't we have one? The unspoken half of this dialogue is that Americans are different. We use tremendously more resources, have many more operations, are fatter, sicker, and have much higher expectations for everything. We are a 10-cylinder, super-charged double turbo fuel-injected culture, and those Swedish national health care plans are for Birkenstock granola four-cylinder types.

The one thing American's don't have an appetite for is taxes, and the enlightened countries with those comprehensive health plans have breathtaking taxes to pay for it all. Now, the presidential candidates say that we will just soak the evil rich for the money and make up for the rest with improved efficiencies, but those arguments are fallacious. There aren't enough rich to soak, and if you think the government will run health care more efficiently - well, that's yet another one of your God-given rights.

So, here goes my theory on the "National Health Service." A basic package of immunizations, well-child care, and health maintenance exams (periodic physical exams, mammograms, colonoscopy at 50, etc.) will be the core of the plan. Emphasis on health maintenance (control of blood pressure, diabetes, smoking cessation, weight control and cancer surveillance) will be paramount. Every health care effort or intervention will be evidence-based; that is, unless there is proof that it is helpful, it won't be provided. So forget the antibiotics for colds, chest X-rays for bronchitis and CT scans for every headache. There will be specific criteria for everything: hip replacement, cataract surgery, coronary bypass surgery, you name it.

68

The only conceivable way to make a national health care plan even remotely feasible will be to control utilization and costs. There will be a certain number of office visits and hospital days and operations available each year, just like England and Canada, and no more. There will be a list of drugs available, and no more. You may wait six months to see a neurologist, and a year or so to get your new hip (assuming you meet the criteria).

This is all very un-American. We treasure our excess eating, fuel consumption, smoking and our world-leading health care utilization. We want it all, and we want it now, and we want it cheap. How can this possibly work? Several things will have to happen.

With rationing of health care (call it whatever you want, that's what it will be) the consumer will need to become patient. When I worked in the VA, the vets there just learned to be patient. They eventually got the care, but realized that it wasn't going to be quick. They also learned that they had to deal with a lot of medical personnel in training, a ponderous system, and an immutable bureaucracy. Once they figured that out, they generally got good care. I liked the VA, actually, because the patients were reasonable and grateful, and understood that I was learning.

I believe there will be a two-tier system. That means that basic services will be offered as part of a National Health Service, and many other services will be considered elective. There will also be the option to opt out of the national system and go to a private provider if you want something in a hurry. It won't be dissimilar to ordering a book from Amazon: four or five days regular mail at no charge, or 20 bucks overnight from FedEx. If you want your hip done next week, you pay, if you want it next year, get in line.

Let's say you feel your knee needs replacing, and the government says it doesn't. You may have the option to do it privately at your own expense. I think that can work. It will lower costs to the government by patients opting out of the system, and give the impatient patient a chance to get what he wants.

If people really value something, they will pay for it. Doctors and health care facilities will also provide more competitively priced packages for cash customers.

The key to a healthy health care system over time is controlling utilization. We use more office visits, ER visits, drugs and operations than any other society. If that health care becomes "free," utilization will mushroom. Utilization will be rationed through a limited number of providers, appointments, OR slots and drug supplies. Only procedures, drugs or therapies shown to have proven efficacy or long-term benefits will be provided through the National Health Service.

Prolonged ICU stays and expensive chemotherapy at the end of life will have to go. There may be restrictions on personal behavior as well: Does the National Health Service pay for repeated vascular reconstructions in smokers? What about recurrent complications of Type II diabetes in the morbidly obese? How many complicated ICU trauma visits does the alcoholic driver get to charge to the public VISA? Is the taxpayer responsible for all the ACL repairs the soccer team racks up during the season? Do I have the right to demand that "everything be done" for my elderly relative with metastatic cancer if I'm not paying the bill?

It is important to understand that in a government-run health care system, the government decides what type of care, how much care and the availability of the care delivered. It will also be supported with substantial additional taxes.

Salaries for health care workers will decline. I would expect Medicare will be rolled into a National Health Service, and that Medicare services will be considerably leaner. There is no way to widen a Medicare-type system, which is already going broke, into a more comprehensive plan.

Do not listen to politicians who tell you we can have comprehensive health care for free. We can have a limited, highly regulated, basic health package with some big tax increases. That may be the most humane, compassionate system we can offer in this society. Most doctors now want some type of universal safety net but do not want to see health care essentially nationalized.

I do think it is essential that a second tier, market-driven element is present in additional to a National Health Service. Allow consumers to pay cash or use private insurance to fund "quality of life" procedures or on-demand office visits. If we believe in a compassionate society, maybe we ought to have a universal health care capability. But if we also believe in a market economy and personal freedom, let those with resources FedEx that office visit for the sore knee and get that nongeneric wonder drug, and let them pay cash. The fact of life is that many very talented physicians are also (gasp!) expecting to be compensated for their expertise and years of training, and government minimum wage won't hold them. A two-tiered system is how Australia, Canada and England hold on to their star doctors.

As a plastic surgeon, I have a few additional suggestions. I think cosmetic surgery should be funded by the government. Why waste all that money on cancer treatment and heart attacks when it only affects that one person? Why should the taxpayer walk around all day, looking at all those lumpy and wrinkled-up people, when it could be prevented? One liposuction can brighten the day of hundreds of people. Don't you think it is your God-given right to look your best? Be sure to write your Congressman or Senator.

Tonsils Away

You can't believe how relieved I am now that one of medicine's dirtiest and darkest secrets has been revealed. I admit I have known about it for years, but have been too afraid to come forward. This is the case of the marauding, child-snatching ear, nose, and throat (ENT) physicians.

Why haven't I come forward? Well, most of them are big guys, the kind that push you down on the playground and steal your Barbie lunch box. (Oops, did I say Barbie? I meant the Hulk).

And if they are willing to snatch children, what would they do to a medical snitch?

Thank heaven it is now in the open. President Obama, in a recent press conference, exposed these mercenaries.

"You come in and you've got a bad sore throat, or your child has a bad sore throat or has repeated sore throats, the doctor may look at the reimbursement system and say to himself, 'You know what? I make a lot more money if I take this kid's tonsils out.'"

You probably didn't know this, but there are laws saying that ENT doctors can't be within 100 feet of a school, because they will snatch children just to take out their tonsils and make money. Watch some morning when they drop their kids off— *they always drop them off a block away.* I'll bet you didn't know that.

Frankly, many specialties do the same thing. I know one orthopedic surgeon who, when he visits his grandmother in the nursing home, takes the little wheels off the walkers of other patients. When they go to use them, they topple over and break their hips. *Ka-ching,* another big dollar Medicare hip replacement.

We do it a lot in plastic surgery. Do you remember those subliminal ads like they used to do in the movie theaters, where it came on the screen so fast that you couldn't see or hear it, but your subconscious would pick it up? *Buy popcorn.* We have ads like that on during Oprah. *You look like a basset hound, you need a facelift. Your rear end is so big, it needs its own area code. Get liposuction.* Stuff like that.

Back to the evil ENT conspiracy. In 1959, there were 1.4 million tonsillectomies in the U.S. We now have more than twice the population, and many more ENT vampires prowling around. And so, accordingly, last year there were, wait, less than 300,000 tonsillectomies. Huh? Over the years, organizations such as the American Academy of Otolaryngology (basically the ENT version of Al Quaeda) have developed things called

72

practice guidelines. They look at all the scientific data for a certain procedure, and they develop rules for who gets what operation. So in tonsillectomy, if you have so many infections treated with antibiotics in a certain time, and it keeps coming back, and the mother is wearing you completely out, then you operate. If those guidelines aren't met, it doesn't matter how bad you want that new ski condo, you don't operate.

The number of coronary bypasses has dropped, not increased. Transurethral resection of the prostate (TURP) has decreased markedly in frequency. Ulcer surgery has practically disappeared. All these were well paying, frequently performed procedures that paid for a lot of boats and golf trips. But, alas, other medicines and procedures came along and replaced the surgery.

If you do an operation without meeting the practice guidelines, the insurance company won't pay for it. If you do an unnecessary operation and something happens, you get sued for sure. Frankly, surgeons are superstitious as well. You do a case just for the money and the Almighty will smite you and your patient. Your Karma will look like three-day-old road kill.

I thought that the stock market crash in 1929 and the Great Depression had led to reforms and regulations to protect the financial system. Look what happened—insolvent banks, massive corporate failures. Don't assume that the government or the "establishment" knows what they are doing.

From the president on down, the people who are about to institute massive changes in your health care system (admittedly, deeply flawed) don't have any idea what they are talking about. They believe whatever the 22-year-old intern whispers in their ear while they are preening in front of the cameras. They continually tout the efficiency of the Faraway Clinic. They have no idea that Montana patients go to the Faraway Clinic, have a big procedure, are quickly discharged, and I take care of the complications for the next six months.

I have yet to hear any of these guys tell us the truth, because it is politically unacceptable. We can't handle the truth. The truth? We are too fat, we are too lazy, we consume way too much health care, we expect something for nothing, and we expect to live forever. We are reckless, we have a constitutional right to our cigarettes, motorcycles, four wheelers, cheeseburgers, knee-tearing sports, Budweisers, and we have got to do it all really fast. And me, I'm right in there with the rest of them. I ignored my blood pressure and cholesterol because I was busy doing unnecessary surgery to make money, and as a result racked up a $36,000 bill for a completely preventable coronary stent. No politician will call me an idiot, but until they do, we aren't going to have meaningful reform.

Whew! After that rant I need to pop open a Bud. Have a good week and watch out for those surgeons. *You look so old, you went to an antique auction and someone bid on you.* President Obama wants to protect you from unnecessary surgery. *Your belly button doesn't collect lint, it collects sweaters.* And it will all be free.

Ma Barker Nearly Meets Her Maker

Ma Barker, at 82, had been slowing down for some time. It turned out that her aortic valve had become very narrow, and I was seeing her, back in my heart surgery days, to discuss valve replacement. Her sons, Junior and Festus, were there for the consultation.

"I dunno," said Junior, stroking his stubbled chin ruminatively, "open heart surgery is a big deal. Mom's had a good life and all, maybe best to let 'er be."

"You idgiot, Junior," remonstrated Festus, "Medicare gonna pay fer it."

"Well then," Junior in full reverse, "let's git 'er done."

Touching. Even I, who have threatened my mother with a nursing home featuring a sweat equity provision, found Ma Barker's story a little chilling.

When I decided to retrain in plastic surgery, I had to uproot my family from their lives, schools, etc.. Feeling guilty, I planned a trip to Disney World as compensation. I signed us up for the Gold Plan, which meant unlimited meals at any of their restaurants. Three meals a day, anything you want, appetizers, desserts—this for a family used to splitting entrées, skipping the soft drinks, and protecting their food from Dad's roving fork. One afternoon, gazing into an aquatic exhibit featuring a particularly corpulent manatee, my little boy said "Daddy, if we keep eating this much, are we going to look like him?"

Our behavior depends greatly on who is paying for what. When I was a broke surgery resident, the other residents and our squeezes would go out and share a pizza and a pitcher. If a drug or equipment rep took us out, it was filet mignon. Guys were throwing back shots of Glenlivet scotch at $35 per. (I, of course, might have had an extra diet Coke.)

Health care is no different than a buffet restaurant. If insurance or Medicare is going to pay for something, our decision process is different than if we are paying for it. Since I do a lot of cosmetic surgery, I have learned this well. I have to figure out how to price procedures so that people will do them, because it is their dime.

Patients that I see who are contemplating things like breast reduction or upper lid blepharoplasty/brow lift for medical indications will frankly tell me that they can only do the procedure if insurance will authorize it.

One of the solutions to the impending Medicare crash and the skyrocketing private insurance costs is placing accountability for health care utilization closer to the consumer. It simply isn't possible for a system like Medicare to allow every member to have two hips, two knees, two cataracts, and a new heart valve without going broke. Which it is. You can see how drastically unpopular politically this approach would be. Elective procedures would have to be cut out of the program. Doctors would then have to put together ultra-efficient packages for those procedures so people could have them done. We can learn a lot from breast implants.

Increasing deductibles for private insurance is one way of reducing utilization. Our family has a 5,000-dollar deductible, so if someone is injured or sick I just tell them to rub some dirt on the problem and suck it up.   Many Medicaid programs have found that even a five-dollar co-pay for ER visits significantly reduces use.

I hate the idea of spending a significantly greater amount of my yacht piggy bank (so far the propeller is paid for) for something as boring as health care. Yuck. But if the country does go broke, we're all done, a has-been like Greece. Survival of our health care system depends on us sharing a pitcher instead of tossing back five shots of Glenlivet. As for doctors, make yourself affordable or learn to like soap operas. We also have to have a mature discussion on end-of-life care instead of yammering about "death squads." Spending 80% of health care dollars on the last year of life will not get us past the propeller stage. I know that if I get more than a cold my family will sell me to a tissue bank while I am still alive. Dad's had a good life.

We get into all kinds of trouble when we deny our basic human nature, which is essentially that of a dog walking on his hind legs. We can't pretend we won't pig out on the Gold Plan. We are creatures of appetite, lust, greed, and avarice. To deny this is to prevent meaningful solutions to our problems. To be aware of and to manage these indecorous impulses lends us our humanity.

What I don't understand is why the insurance company won't pay for my hair transplants. I am likely to catch a cold.

Chapter 7
It Couldn't Happen to a Nicer Patient

One minute life is fine, the next you are missing a chunk of your ear or your foot. Among the most interesting aspects of plastic surgery are the complex reconstructions of body parts, as well as the patients attached (or not) to them.

~~~~~~

It's Never Too Late

Among the many hackneyed expressions that lurk in our language is "it's never too late."

It is probably too late for me to be, as I had always assumed I would be, quarterback of the Dallas Cowboys. As a boy I thought Dandy Don Meredith was the coolest ever. As recent as 2005 I was quarterback of the University of Mississippi Surgery Department football team, throwing six touchdowns with only 15 interceptions, none of which was actually my fault. But at 53, I would be older than even Brett Farve by a few months, so it may be getting a little late for an NFL career.

Each year, Time magazine publishes an article called "The World's Ten Worst Dictators." My mom always calls me when the issue comes out, because she knows I always wanted to be a dictator (not president, I couldn't handle Congress and the Supreme Court), and it is hard not being included. With two kids in college, and another coming up, it is going to be tough to get my dictator career going.

My father was born with and lived most of his life with prominent ears. One Christmas I came home from college, and I couldn't figure out why he looked different. At age 63, when finances finally permitted, he finally had his ears fixed. He might have been the world's oldest otoplasty patient, but in his mind it definitely wasn't too late.

I recently had a patient who presented for breast reconstruction 19 years after her mastectomy. She told me that she had thought that you either had to do it right away or not at all. She learned otherwise, and after years of prostheses and struggling with clothes, she thought she would look into it. We are in the process of a reconstruction with a latissimus dorsi flap, which is skin and muscle from the back combined with an implant.

Anyone who has dealt with breast cancer knows how intense the experience can be. On Monday you have a mammogram, and Tuesday you get a call saying there is abnormality. There is an ultrasound-guided biopsy on Wednesday, and Thursday or Friday you are sitting in a doctor's office discussing a finding of cancer. Within a week you see a surgeon, an oncologist, and maybe a plastic surgeon. Each presents a semester's worth of medical information.

The most common method of treating breast cancer is with what is termed breast conservation therapy. That means the tumor is removed (the elegantly named "lumpectomy") and then, in most cases, radiation treatment to the breast.

In some cases, however, complete removal of the breast, mastectomy, is chosen. There may be multiple tumors, a strong genetic risk of more tumors, or an unusually large tumor. Some patients choose mastectomy

Reconstruction can be immediate, at the time of the surgery, or delayed, which means anytime from months to apparently 19 years. Immediate reconstruction has the advantage of consolidating the number of operations and not waking up with the mastectomy defect. The disadvantages are that you have to make yet another set of decisions in a short time, and there is a possibility that your treatment plan will change after surgery. Sometimes intraoperative findings, such as involved lymph nodes, will necessitate radiation therapy, which can be unkind to our artistry.

What is critical in this process is to not feel pressured when you are already a nervous wreck. If you are comfortable and confident in your care plan, go for it. If not, pester the doctors and their posse until you are comfortable, or else delay not the cancer treatment itself but the decisions about what to do with the shape and size of the breast. You might want to consider lifting or changing the size of the uninvolved breast to get a better match with the reconstructed one.

Breast reconstruction is an insurance or Medicare/Medicaid covered expense by federal law. They don't cover hair transplants for excessively virile plastic surgeons.

Breast reconstruction is my favorite thing to do, because it requires creativity and artistry within the confines of skin and muscle and blood supply. Sure, Michelangelo did nice breasts, but marble gets cold when you are up skiing in the mountains. The relationships I develop with my patients during the education and surgical process are among the most satisfying in medicine. Many of the patients are having immediate reconstruction, but perhaps more have gone through the treatment process and are now able to focus completely on reconstruction, even if months or years have gone by.

It may, in fact, be too late to be an NFL quarterback or a top ten dictator. But I did do a reconstruction on a 75 year old woman, and I know it sounds nuts at first, but she said "I'm fit and active and my parents lived to 95, so other than your obsolescent age prejudice, why shouldn't you do me? " Yes ma'am.

We fix what we can, and release what we can't. It is the things that we can fix, but won't—the ancient slight, the lingering grudge, the felt but unspoken sentiment—whose corrosive waves lap relentlessly at our well-being, that we must act on before it is too late. Someone may die, a valuable relationship is lost to pride, or an opportunity is fearfully shirked.

Where are my pads and spikes?

Sometimes You Get Snipped

Betrayal is a shocking, disheartening, and disorienting experience.

A coworker you thought you could trust steals all the credit for a group project.

You see someone else's truck parked in front of your girlfriend's house—at 3 a.m.

That piece of leftover rib eye you've been thinking about all day is gone from the refrigerator when you get home.

Pam and Barb run a horse training operation in Red Lodge. Pam was hooking up the hose to fill a big water tank. Among the horses milling about was Cash, a three-year-old stallion.

"All of a sudden I felt this tearing sensation on my right ear," Pam recalls. "I think Cash thought my sunglasses were some sort of a treat, because he bit my ear off." Even after thirty years of surgery, that even grosses me out.

Pam wasn't exactly sure at the time what had happened, just that there seemed to be a lot of blood. She walked up to the barn to have Barb take a look.

Barb was impressed. "He bit your ear off," Barb told Pam.

"Put some pressure on that and let's try to find the ear."

Barb went to the tank, "kind of sifted through the grass in the water", and sure enough, found the ear. Actually, about half the ear, the outside portion with the curve.

When I met them, they had the part nicely packaged in a Zip-Lock, and were remarkably sanguine about the whole thing. The ear was missing from the top of the helix, the top curvy thing, down to the lobe. Fortunately, the inside curve (antihelix) and the bowl (concha) were still there. I explained that we would reconstruct the rim of the ear with a tube of skin from behind

80

the ear. You can't sew ears back on (it's tempting, everyone's tried it, never works due to lack of blood supply) but I did peel the skin off the cartilage, put the cartilage inside my skin tube, and made a passable ear. You have to leave the two ends of the tube attached to the head for a few weeks until the skin grows into the ear.

About a month later we divided the skin tube, tuned up the shape a little, and there you go.

Pam is also trained as a social worker, and is interested in equine therapy, which is sort of like being a horse shrink. I was fascinated to see how she would work things out with the offending Cash. Would they do couples therapy, group counseling, anger management, how could they get through this?

Pam was confident there would be resolution.

"How?" I wondered.

"He's getting snipped."

"Snipped?"

"Yeah. Gelded. That's where they cut....."

I got the idea. Forgiveness is a transcendent act of humanity. It separates us from the beasts. New Testament versus Old. To forgive an act of betrayal requires the most profound understanding of the egoistic, atavistic darkness that inhabits all of our souls.

Or not. So it is best to be careful. Sometimes you aren't forgiven. Sometimes you get snipped.

Don't Shoot Yourself In The Foot

There were these three guys in a truck—a preacher, a cowboy, and a plumber. Which one shot himself in the foot?

Perry Wolt, the plumber, still isn't sure exactly how he blew a hole the size of a beer can in the top of his foot.

"I was unloading my Remington 7 mm mag, moving it from one hand to another, when it went off. You've read about some of those Remingtons going off, trigger problems." At this point Perry's wife chimed in. "Don't blame the gun."

Perry looked down after the blast and saw shredded boot, blood, and chunks of bone. "I knew I was in trouble. Twenty miles from town." Town being Roundup.

I had to ask. "No," Perry answered, "I wasn't drunk, or even drinking." I assume most of my trauma patients—car wrecks, shootings, stabbings, etc.—are drunk. Come to think of it, my last trauma patient wasn't drunk, technically. If you overlook the oxycodone, valium, meth, and pot, that is. But Perry was clean.

Dr. Rob Schultz, a Billings Clinic Orthopedic surgeon, cleaned up the mess, sorted out the chunky ankle soup, and called me. "Gonna need a free flap," was his opinion.

A free flap is used when you need a major piece of meat to fill a major hole somewhere. In this case, we needed muscle to provide both coverage of the exposed bone and a blood supply to nurture the bone grafts that Rob was going to be putting in place of the bone lying on the ground twenty miles from Roundup.

In Perry's case, we took part of his right abdominal muscle, the rectus abdominus, along with the artery and vein that supplies the muscle. We then sewed that artery and vein to the artery and vein behind Perry's ankle, hooking up the muscle to a blood supply, in the process putting a nice piece of juicy steak in the yawning hole. We then place a skin graft over the muscle. What a cool case.

I will not be showing pictures of Perry's foot to my cosmetic surgery patients. That is one ugly foot. There are big pins sticking in the bones, and a serious lump of meat that hasn't shrunk yet. But it should walk, plumb, and hunt.

So what do you think of this, Perry? "I think, in a way, that the Good Lord sat me down for a while. I was being very impatient, throwing tantrums, being obnoxious. I think he's teaching me to be patient." If the image of the Lord packing an elk rifle isn't enough to keep you in line, I don't know what is.

I am struck by how moments of impatience, of distraction, can change our lives. Fiddling with a radio or cellphone in the car. Spacing off handling a weapon. A little too much reach on a ladder. Neglecting the helmet or seatbelt. An extra drink. Driving your car into the downtown parking garage with its stupid low ceiling, forgetting that you put the luggage carrier on top. Docking a chartered yacht in a covered slip and not checking to see if the ridiculously high satellite dish would fit under the roof.

Once again life boils down to a football analogy. Avoid stupid turnovers. Pay attention to the simple stuff. There's cancer, heart disease, climate change, tsunamis, adolescent children, and tax auditors all out to get you—you don't need to help.

Any advice Perry? "Yeah. Don't shoot yourself in the foot."

You Gotta Serve Somebody

In the early nineties a number of young surgeons arrived in Billings—early thirties types dripping with surgical testosterone, and we formed a basketball team to compete in the Y leagues. We played in the "C" or the "B" leagues, which are known for the barely controlled mayhem resembling prison ball.

A frequent opponent was a team from a local company, whose identity will remain obscure. The two teams were fairly evenly matched—slightly over-the-hill but still obstreperous men working out the frustrations of the day in sanctioned bodily assault. Our games were contentious, chippy, and not infrequently bloody, many of them adjudicated by James, a long suffering Y referee who marveled at the infantile behavior of those who would take his life in their hands should he be in a car wreck.

I will call him Stewie. I always had to guard Stewie. They had three guys I couldn't guard at all, so I got Stewie, who was bigger than I and probably better in general. To compensate, I may have, at times, possibly, grabbed his shirt, stepped on his foot, and otherwise impeded his progress in order to prevent him from punking me completely. This aroused a certain degree of enmity in Stewie, who rather uncharitably called me "dirty", accompanied by a look of such malevolence that I always hung near my teammates after the games. This was not helped by the fact that we occasionally brought ringers to play with us, medical reps who played a little college ball and such.

So one winter I was called to see a young man who had an empyema, a serious infection in the lung cavity where a collection of pus gets trapped between the lung and the ribs. This guy, whose diagnosis was delayed probably by a week, was sick as a mutt—fever, couldn't eat, short of breath, horrible cough.

I walked in the room and at first didn't recognize him. He looked near dead. At about the same time, we recognized each other. Awkward is not remotely adequate to describe the discomfort. But Stewie wasn't Stewie, he was beaten and sick and fearful. Rather than addressing the obvious, I simply told him what we needed to do and that we would do it quickly. He just nodded.

Draining pus leads to miracles. After surgery, Stewie moped for a day or two, then on the third day I came in on rounds and there he was, sitting up, with that same malevolent stare. "I appreciate what you did and all," he said in a low, Clint-like murmur, "but this changes nothing." I understood.

One of the cool things about practicing in a smaller community is being able to help people you know. I think I've operated on most of the husbands of my mom's sorority house. I did an aortic valve on a lady one time who said she had held me at my baby shower. I sew up the kids who get split in basketball games, and clean up after car wrecks and fights. Satisfaction can be great and so can be the pressure—operating on a friend's child—I'd rather have a last second kick in the Super Bowl.

84

The underlying theme in health care, or really in any professional endeavor, has to be service. Whether you're on the loading dock at the hospital or in the operating room, working nights in the nursing home, or toiling in some clinic a hundred miles from Nowhere, serving others needs to be at the core of what you do. It seems to me that so many people are struggling for meaning in their lives. I have the usual frustrations of a sex symbol/rock star/Hollywood plastic surgeon, but meaning isn't one of them, because when I patch a hole in a paraplegic's backside or reconstruct a breast in a cancer patient, I am serving someone. That's easy, you might say, when you are in such a position, and that's true to some extent. But service is an attitude applicable to any field or job or location. Are you teaching your younger colleagues, supporting your older ones, enriching those around you, or are you taking life away from the system in which you function?

Bob Dylan summarizes this well

You may be a businessman or some high-degree thief
They may call you Doctor or they may call you Chief
But you're gonna have to serve somebody, yes indeed
You're gonna have to serve somebody

The next year, on the court at the Y, Stewie was there. Rather than display any gratitude, he ran over me on drives, jumped over my back, and generally destroyed me. I eyed the left side of his rib cage, where I knew that incision was, and drew back my elbow......but then he was gone, and late again, I scurried after.

Chapter 8
The Business of Medicine

As much as some practitioners like to believe they are high priests of the healing arts, medicine is as much a business as any other field, with just as much silliness.

~~~~~~~~~~~~~~~~~~~~~~~~~~~~~~~~~~

Our New Home

I never bought into the whole "sharing" thing as a child. If it was tasty, why not eat the whole thing? If an activity was fun, why "take turns?" Sharing was "nice". "It's nice to share." My idea of sharing is to eat all of mine and part of yours. My children grew up with one protective arm curled around their plate, prison-style.

My decent, God-fearing parents tried to bring me up right. They taught me that there was, presumably, some sort of deferred, karmic benefit from sharing. To me, that was a cynical play on the part of someone who wanted half your ice cream bar. Ten years of shark infested surgical residency reinforced that belief.

Thus the difficulty when my office functions not only as a work cubicle, but as the bathroom and storeroom as well. For someone to get by to use the bathroom, I have to squash my chest against my desk so they can squeeze by. If I leave my chair for more than a few minutes, it is piled with an empty box, a stack of supplies, or a piece of unused equipment. Since my office is also essentially in the middle of the only corridor, everyone can tell when I am looking at yacht porn on the computer.

Our office was designed for one doctor working a reasonable schedule. There are two of us cranking 60 hours a week. Time for another space.

The options are to rent a larger medical space, which is really expensive, or to build your own, which is hideously expensive. Since our cosmetic surgery patients really don't care to tramp through a public arena the day after a facelift, we needed something private with rear parking, which meant we had to build. Since we also do a lot of reconstructive surgery close to the hospitals, we needed to be close. The logical move was to buy a gas station.

We loved the location at 17th and Poly, but you can imagine the environmental ramifications of tearing down a gas station. I thought we could burn it down and therefore take care of any potential residual gas and oil. No one else thought that.

We told the architect what we wanted and what our budget was. My focus was on the upstairs man cave, with the recliners, flat screen tuned to ESPN, and frosty G & T waiting for the long early evening dictation sessions. As it turned out, we were only 1.2 million over budget, which meant I could retire in 2051, assuming I sold my house, lived in the office, and ate bulk mac and cheese.

So we learned a new term: "value engineering". This means cutting out all the good stuff. If you have built a house, you know what I mean. Out with the granite, in with the Formica. The design team gently explained that the man cave, indeed the whole second floor as well as the basement, would have to go. All the essential medical stuff and patient care areas were spared--yawn.

When I pushed them about some of the goodies, the architect started doodling a urinal on the plans of my office, so I backed off.

The regulations for medical construction are something else. Everything is super wide, so you can drive a semi truck down the halls and around the operating table. There must be a bathroom for every patient. Safety and infection control are obsessions, so I have to be hosed down between patients.

Overall it has been a fascinating and scary process. This isn't exactly the kind of economic climate that makes you excited about a major financial adventure.

Primarily, we want to do a better job for our patients. We're cramped, and we keep people waiting longer than a reasonable period because of space limitations. Access for wheelchairs and stretchers is limited.

There is another, more philosophical issue at work as well. This community supports our practice. Everyone involved in our building we know in some capacity, mostly through kids' activities, and they have businesses and employees too. We could sit on our resources, not borrow a donkey cart of money, and ride out whatever we're calling this economic flu. This not only leaves me stuck in the bathroom, dodging empty boxes, but also tells the community that I don't think there is much of a future here.

A lot of construction in this area now is medical—two new cancer centers, the OB-GYN place out west, a planned peds clinic, and the arthritis clinic on Broadwater. Both hospitals have nice new ERs. No question there is a lot of money in medicine, much of it derived from your misfortune, but medical dollars in this community get recycled in a big way to plumbers, electricians, sheet rockers, and man cave whackers.

Maybe it is nice after all to share, and to be nice. Nah. It's nice not to have a bathroom as your office. I'll work on the sharing later.

Electric Dreams

There are words and phrases that swirl like lacerating Arctic winds through our chest, descending to our diaphragms in a clutch of dread.

The boss says "come in my office and close the door."

Your doctor calls and says "I'd like you to come in to review your CAT scan, better bring your wife."

Your son says "Dad, I'm thinking of becoming a trial attorney." That kind of stuff.

There are, however, no more terrifying words, heard in your business, hospital, government agency, or wherever you earn your daily bread, than "we are getting a new computer system."

"But we just got a new computer system," you protest. Yeah, and that unemployed kid in your basement with the Master's degree is still in second grade.

"Maybe I could just retire." Sure, that would work; if your retirement plan didn't look like the rudder of the Titanic just before it snuggled between a couple of icebergs.

Both of our local hospitals have made the move to the hippest of the hip, the coolest of the cool, everyone's all-encompassing political solution to rising health care costs and dandruff—the electronic medical record.

No more doctors' handwriting. No more quick notes or orders.

Sigh.

If you have patients on several different floors in the hospital, or more than one hospital, you have to first locate, and then sign into a computer on each floor. User name and password is a duo reminiscent to me of herpes and cancer.

My son and his homies are connoisseurs of complex video games—multiple layers of strategy, tactics, storylines, and maneuvers. The other night they picked up a new game, fiddled with it for a few minutes, and despite no documentation, training seminars, or helpful facilitators flown in from Denver, were off and running. For instance, let's say you wish to eliminate a particularly vexatious opponent, the guy who took you out with an M-16 in the last episode. A bazooka won't satisfy; you're torqued, you need to get personal. The boys know intuitively that a combination of the left toggle switch and the right blue button will allow them to move in close to the enemy and deploy a chain saw. (My obvious failure as a parent is beyond the scope of this discussion.)

The X-box guys do not write hospital software. The most important and frequently used icons on the screen in medical software will be the smallest and most improbably named. Instead of a button that says "do you want to do the same lame stuff you usually do?" I have to build a problem list, initiate, reconcile medications, initiate, oh yeah, and refresh, write transfer orders, refresh, initiate, blah, blah, blah. Then the nurse calls and says "why didn't you do orders, didn't you finalize?" Finalize. Where's the bazooka, or better yet, the chainsaw?

This last Saturday morning I spent building my "favorites list", which is apparently the key to efficiency with these programs. I selected, checked, saved, accepted, labeled, then discarded and cancelled. "Oh yeah," my son said, "The hot key. That's the red button."

I think this will all be okay. If nothing else I'll be able to read what other doctors say, which to this point has been a hieroglyphic enigma. We will all figure it out, although I still can't find a way to get one of my yacht-porn websites under "favorites."

I am by no means a technophobe. I had the very first IBM PC with the big floppies, remember those, you old people? But a concern niggles at me. I used to come on a patient floor and couldn't find a nurse or therapist, because they were in patient rooms. Now they are all ensconced in front of banks of monitors, their visages rapt in worship of the God of Documentation.

Most patients just want a comfortable bed, a little ice in their water pitcher, edible food, and their Percocet on time. Oh yeah, and someone with a comforting touch in a time of fear and vulnerability.

I don't think there is any question that documentation, billing, and accessibility of records are improved with these systems. Improved patient care? We'll see.

Let's see. I'm 54 now, what are the chances I'll have to learn a new system after these? I'm pretty good on our office computer system, barely adequate at Billings Clinic, and new at the St. Vincent one. Since we have decided to let a bunch of C league political hacks in Greece and Italy run the US economy, it looks like I'll have to endure another round of software surprise, only next time with significantly more holes in my brain. I'll have to tattoo my user name and password on the back of one hand, and a diagram of a breast augmentation on the back of the other.

Acceptance of change is a hallmark of youth and intellectual flexibility. When you no longer have a hot button, you're done. No, make that finalized.

Out of Town

You learn all kinds of stuff when you read the newspaper. A few weeks ago the Gazette carried an article in the Health section about US citizens seeking surgical procedures in foreign countries (*High costs send patients overseas for medical care*, Jan. 10). Instead of paying over $200,000 to have a heart valve operation at Duke, the patient quoted in the article had the procedure performed in India for $6500, which also included an oil change and vacuuming. Apparently the hospital in India was beautiful and clean and the service was great.

On January 1st, another Gazette article profiled my retired senior partner, Dr. Walt Peet (*Retired Plastic Surgeon Helps Those in Need*, Jan. 1). He described a mission trip to India to repair cleft lips and palates. I spoke to Walt after his return, and he related the challenge of doing complex surgery with primitive equipment in squalid facilities.

Yet another wire service article reported the fact that although India was in the midst of dramatic economic growth, half of the children there were malnourished. I've always suspected that a deep sense of irony was a requirement to be a newspaper editor.

I don't doubt that you can get heart surgery, liposuction, a new hip, or a sex change operation overseas for a bargain, including an attractive tote bag with a set of Ginsu knives inside. I'm not going to debate the quality of the care delivered in these places, because I don't really know. But let's take a broader look at the "social contract" and what constitutes the kind of society in which we wish to live.

Let's say, for the purposes of argument, that you are a drunk 19 year old screaming down the wrong side Grand Avenue at 80 miles an hour on your Kawasaki at 2 a.m., and, bummer, you hit a one ton Dodge Ram head on. Or, you are a two month old baby with a cleft lip and palate and your mommy is a meth head in jail. Perhaps you are a hard working but uninsured forty five year old that has a sudden heart attack. What kind of medical care will you get?

The answer is that you will get the best, state of the art, care available. The above three cases will likely generate over a million dollars of hospital, physician, and long term care charges that will never be paid. Health insurance premiums will go up, taxes will rise to cover the Medicaid costs, and charges will rise to cover the deficit. But as a society, we are unwilling to let people go without care, for which we should be rightfully proud. The countries that offer discount medical tourism don't do things that way. They let poor kids live with gross deformities and let them go hungry while cheerfully collecting cash from Americans. Compassion is expensive.

Let's take another angle. There is a high volume auto dealer in Idaho that offers great prices on new vehicles. Many Montanans (including the incumbent governor) have purchased vehicles there. I have not. Why? Because every time I look around, I see Underriner sponsoring the symphony, Bob Smith doing Summerfair, and Denny Menholt supporting MSU-B. Our office could buy office products online, but Frank Cross at Reporter paid 500 bucks for a green cake made by a high school boy at a Billings Catholic School auction. Medical care is big business in Billings, employing thousands, driving the economy, and most importantly, taking care of us when we need it the most.

What about quality? I have heard "Ooh, I need heart surgery, that's a big deal; I should go to the Mayo Clinic or the Texas Heart Institute." Here's the reality. Although fine institutions, they are training hospitals, and your heart surgery may be performed by someone who is quite possibly doing their *first* heart surgery. Or, you could stay in Billings and have your heart surgery done in top-ranked hospitals by a *graduate* of one of those programs, the difference being that Drs. Dernbach or Millikan or Winton have done *thousands* of heart operations. These guys will also be there to hold your hand and take care of a problem if there is one. If you have a complication and your surgeon is thousands of miles away, then what?

How about sneaking off to Vegas for a breast augmentation or a face lift?

I could make the argument that the cosmetic boys in Vegas don't take care of Billings trauma victims or kids with congenital deformities. I could say "try calling a Vegas cosmetic surgeon when your kid cracks open his head at two in the morning", but I won't (or maybe I just did). But that aside, some folks worry about confidentiality. They don't want anyone to know they have had cosmetic surgery. I can assure you that *all kinds* of people you know have had cosmetic surgery in Billings and you don't know it, because we are exquisitely careful about confidentiality.

Price is always a consideration. Some high volume operators in larger areas offer low prices, but at the cost of personal attention and follow-up. By the time travel costs are thrown in, it isn't a deal at all. What if you have a complication? Who pays for it? Do you go back to Vegas? Finally, marginal surgeons hide in big places, and often the only thing they do well is market. If you aren't good in a smaller town, you are gone quickly.

Out of town medical care is a complex issue. Our community supports, enriches, and sustains us. As individuals, we must do the same for our community. In the end, all altruism aside, we want the best care. After having worked in over thirty hospitals in four major universities, when I or a member of my family needs it done right, it will be done right here.

I Operate On Badger 5

I have to tell you about a great operation I did last week. I wandered out to the kitchen in the middle of the night, parched from one of those low humidity Montana winter nights, and found a large puddle of water on the floor. An investigation revealed a crack in the garbage disposal.

The diagnosis being made, the therapeutic plan was designed. The culprit garbage disposal was a "Badger 5", and miraculously, the hardware store actually carried the same model. I gathered up the tools, remembered to turn off the water and electricity to the unit (talk about bad complications) and got to work.

I think my wife kind of enjoys it when I play handyman, lingering unnecessarily while I'm under the sink, then, when I'm done saying "gee, sir, I'm a little short of cash this month, do you have any.....payment plans?" That sort of thing. Anyway, the disposal successfully roaring, I instinctively moved to the phone to dictate an operative report. Then I realized *I don't have to*. Not only that, I didn't have to hand write an operative note, write postop orders (feed the disposal only liquids the first two days), no progress notes, and no discharge summary. The medical reconciliation form, the patient instruction form, the nursing home transfer orders, and the Medicare medical necessity form—the Badger 5 needed not a one. Nor will I receive a phone call or snippy email from the coding department wanting to know what kind of wrench I used, because I forgot to dictate that in my operative report. Again.

I'm getting to like the Badger 5. So far, Badger 5 hasn't sent me a five-page form from work requesting a statement regarding the nature of the medical disability, and then listing which of the following 12,000 tasks the Badger 5 can or cannot do. (Can grind up bananas, no on the beer cans.) There is no five-page form from the short-term disability company asking why, since the patient had a mole removal, they need two months off work. Badger 5 worked the minute I put him in.

I don't need any privileges to work under my sink. The two hospitals just sent me privilege renewal forms, both small novels. There are pages of questions to be filled out. "Have you been arrested since your last application?" "Do you use illicit drugs?" (Oh, sure, let me tell you all about it) "How many times have you visited the Ocean Alexander Yachts website in the last month?" "Have you ever wanted to harm a hospital administrator, and if so, are you packing?" "Do you wear women's lingerie under your scrub suit?" (That's none of their business. If a person feels more confident wearing a lace teddy while sewing arteries, well, never mind.)

Just in the last few months, we now have to sign all pathology and laboratory request slips and provide a five-digit diagnosis code. Most all operations require a letter requesting preauthorization from the insurance company, not to mention a detailed history and physical dictation, a consent form, a preoperative order form, and a form attesting that I have had less than three drinks before driving to the hospital.

Three boards of surgery certify me, all of which require glutinous meals of paper annually. I fill out peer review forms on my peers' screw-ups, as they do mine. The most important form, the insurance form (the part where I get paid) is surely going to be fired right back at me for some perceived mistake, so they can pay me six months later.

Much of the impetus for all this paperwork is the fraud perpetrated by some of our medical brethren. Some doctor in New York City collected 2.8 million bucks from Medicare, which is truly amazing, since Medicare pays me about $19.99 to do a four-hour operation. (But wait, there's more.) This character is a true genius, a Mozart of fraud, billing something like 15,000 procedures in a family practice setting *in one year*. Despite the fact that my paperwork now doubles, you have to admire that sort of virtuosity. I hope the judge sentences her to a life sentence of filling out forms.

We all deal with paperwork, it isn't specific to medicine, and I am sure the folks who dream up all these forms have their reasons. Of course, so did the Spanish Inquisition. But I'm pretty sure the average nurse spends more time in front of a hospital computer now than at the bedside, and every minute in my day that I spend on mindless scribble has to come from somewhere, such as chatting with my patient about their son's clueless basketball coach.

The Badger 5 grinds away without complaint. But the Badger 5 won't make me cookies, or tell me a joke, or take my hand, tearfully, and thank me for making him whole again. To have those moments in life, in your job, is truly a privilege, and if the price of that is a mountain of paper, then I shall continue my climb.

The List

I looked at the list, first scanning it quickly, then more slowly.

My initial suspicion was confirmed. I wasn't on it.

Face it; we all like to be included. To make the lists—the guys who made the team, the kids invited to the birthday party, Billings Sexiest Plastic Surgeon Alive—is to be one of the Cool.

I felt a little let down.

This list was in the November 20, 2011 Billings Gazette. The article was on a new law requiring all medically related companies to report any payments to doctors. There was quite a list of physicians who received meals, money, trips, etc. for various activities promoting treatments or drugs.

The article discussed concerns that such honoraria might influence physician choices regarding products or treatments.

The physicians responded that they were providing educational services that required their time and resources. I didn't really care because I was sulking. Apparently no one thought my influence worth, well, anything.

Back in my heart surgery days, I went to a meeting in San Diego pertaining to valve surgery. After a teaching session during the day, one of the reps for a valve company invited me to "a little get-together" that evening. He told me to be in front of the hotel at 6 pm.

Right on time, a black Town Car arrived, just for me, and we took off. To Sea World. They had rented Sea World. The whole thing.

About every fifty feet at Sea World was a different "restaurant" under a tent—Indian food, Italian, you name it. About every ten feet was a full bar. We ate gourmet food, drank expensive booze, and had a personal performance by Shamu. I had to admit, my feelings toward this particular valve were very warm. I thought their 500,000 dollars, the cost of this reception, was well spent.

Once I got home, though, I continued to use another valve. The Shamu valve has a single leaf, and the two-leaf valve seems to have more favorable hemodynamic characteristics. My patients also complained that the Shamu valve made too much noise. I think the rep who took me to Sea World was understandably miffed.

Don't get me wrong. I have nothing against bribes. My current price is 6.25 million. I need about 1.25 million for the yacht, then the other five for marina fees, diesel, insurance, maintenance, food, and booze. My policy is one bribe only, though, because like my hero and role model Richard Nixon, I am not a crook. The problem is, I can't even make a lousy list in Billings MT.

I met with a drug representative a few weeks ago about a new pain medication. This one was supposed to avoid the problems with narcotics (nausea, itching, addiction) and work better than the non-narcotic meds. So I wrote a prescription, and about a half-hour later got a call from my patient. "Are you nuts, doc, this stuff is ninety-three bucks. You're killing me. I'll take whiskey for the pain."

There's no question that these medical companies spend money for a reason, and I don't have any problem with the disclosure requirement, other than I find it embarrassing that no one feels I am worth bribing. If you honestly think your behavior and judgment are beyond reproach, then who cares who knows.

Almost all of our prescribing practices are set by outside factors. For one thing, most patients, or mine anyway, are pretty savvy. They want and demand generic drugs, and so most all of the drugs I use are generic. Insurance companies, Medicare, Medicaid, and the hospitals have formularies, which are the lists of drugs from which you have to choose. No wiggle there.

I use some very expensive devices and products for reconstructive surgery. I have some very friendly relationships with the vendors who supply them. But these guys know that if their competitor gives the patient and hospital an equivalent product for less money, there's no incentive (short of 6.25 million) that will help. I want to be seen as an efficient and low cost provider, in addition to the Sexiest Billings Plastic Surgeon Alive.

What does seem to help the companies is appealing directly to the consumer. "Ask your doctor about Titan XL, a new drug for erectile dysfunction." I just love direct to consumer drug marketing. "Daddy, what is erectile dysfunction? What does the drug do, Daddy?" No, honey, Daddy doesn't want Titan XL for Christmas. Not this Christmas.

We all have to get smarter about health care costs. Our current model is to wander into the bar with a credit card and order everything on the menu.

So, I pledge to you, as a representative of the medical community, that despite meals, trips, cash honoraria, and personal Shamu audiences, we will make decisions based only on what is best and least expensive for our patients. Unless someone can come up with 6.25 million. Then I'll say or do anything.

Chapter 9
Plastique

Plastic Surgery is more full of misconception, hype, and baloney than any other medical specialty. Rather than get frustrated with the trivializing of an important profession, I've decided to roll with the fun.

My Own Reality Show

Television shows with a medical theme have been among the most successful vehicles in entertainment history. Take "MASH," which generated monster ratings and revenue, and lives on in syndication. Current hits such as "House," "ER" and "Grey's Anatomy," among many, reflect the viewer's fascination with life in the medical world.

No doubt you have heard physicians complain about these shows. You'll see scenes of patients in private rooms having intense conversations while a respirator runs full tilt next to them. Interns do everything from run MRI scanners to performing brain surgery, all in one episode. Rare diseases seem to be exceedingly common. Some doctors use this type of anecdotal evidence to say that medical shows are just plain silly.

I disagree. I am dictating this article as I head up Zimmerman Trail in my Lamborghini Murcielago, going about 80, and I'll ramp this baby up to about 120 on Highway 3 on my way to work. No worries about Highway Patrol, they know they can't catch me. My bulging pectoralis major muscles enjoy the brush of the Italian silk shirts I favor, and my tan, taut skin barely contains the biceps brachii resting on the open window. The wind courses through my dark, espresso-colored hair, thick as a wire brush, styled once a week by this guy (I think it's a guy, hard to tell) who flies in from L.A.

I'll stop at the hospital first. I have a few patients there - Siamese twins I have separated in miracle operations, Mafia informants who needed new faces, and in general patients who have had never-before-performed-life-saving-one-in-a-million-chance operations that turned out perfectly. You know the drill - remove the bandages, speechless amazement followed by grateful sobs. It all gets a bit much sometimes, especially if they slobber on the Armani. First, I must navigate the hallways full of young, hot nurses trying to drag me into those innumerable empty rooms that all hospitals have. I have instructed the hospital administration that ONLY young, hot nurses in uniforms two sizes too small work on my floor; put all the old, mom-with-three-kids ones on orthopedics or medicine or somewhere like that.

Of course, I resist all these advances, as I am a good family man. I have been happily married for more than eight months to my, uh, let's see, I guess it's my fourth wife, who my accountant says better be the one to last a lifetime. I met her at my daughter's soccer game, and when they both scored two goals, I figured that was a cosmic sign.

So it's on to the office, a palatial structure of marble, crystal and burnished titanium. The office is also stocked with babes, who we don't actually pay with money but rather with implants. Their only job is to look good. In the back, we have a bunch of old, smart business people and nurses who do all the work but don't get on camera when we do our local reality TV series

"Magic City Makeover." I expect you will be seeing this show on the networks soon, as my "Brazilian Tush Tuck" is attracting international attention.

So as you can see, the TV shows get it pretty close after all. The whining you hear is from doctors who aren't young and sexy and have boring lives taking care of busted hips and high blood pressure and other kinds of icky smelly stuff. The only thing that really gets me is the way those shows make out like doctors have these big, inflated egos. That is just way off.

Certifiable

There have been a couple of widely reported deaths in the last few months in patients who have had cosmetic surgery. One was the mother of Kanye West, a rap artist, and the other a teenage girl who had breast augmentation in Florida. These sort of events send a chill through anyone facing surgery, and a big chill through the innards of plastic surgeons. Why did these events occur and what can we learn from them?

Donde West, the rapper's mom, underwent a combination of a belt lipectomy and a breast augmentation. A belt lipectomy is like a tummy tuck but goes all the way around the body, like a lower body "lift." The two procedures took about six hours, and she was discharged home that evening. Although she was up and around that evening, she complained of chest pains and shortness of breath the next day. She apparently suffered a cardiac arrest that evening and died. An autopsy showed coronary artery disease. There were no apparent surgical mistakes. Her surgeon, a Dr. Adams, had been featured on "Oprah."

West was 58 years old and had a history of hypertension. Her sister had died of a heart attack. West was described in the coroner's report as a borderline diabetic. She was African-American, and she was obese. She did not receive a preoperative clearance from an internist, and had no preoperative stress testing or cardiac evaluation.

One of the constant themes in board examinations when you want to be certified by the American Board of Plastic Surgery is safety. When you take the oral examination, you are in a room with three very mean examiners who have all trained at Guantanamo Bay. Besides applying electric current to your teeth and pliers to your eyelids, there are many, many interrogations about patient safety. For instance, they will give you a scenario such as "a 58-year-old African-American female with hypertension, borderline diabetes, and a family history of sudden cardiac death wants a tummy tuck," and if you don't say, "the first thing I would do is ask for a stress test from her internist," it is straight to the waterboard. You flunk. Board exams are not about how you put in breast implants or suck fat. They are about seeing if you are a safe surgeon.

Well, Oprah's boy was not board-certified. Somewhere along the line he didn't jump the hoops. Yeah, he is good-looking and advertises a lot and he was on "Oprah." But was he well-versed in preoperative assessment of risk? Was he really thinking about the advisability of doing a big combo procedure and sending the lady home that night? I can tell you those board examiners think a lot about that stuff, and they think about what they can do to you if you don't know it.

What about the girl in Florida? She had what appeared to be an uneventful breast augmentation, and then developed malignant hyperthermia, which is a condition where a patient who has undergone general anesthesia develops a very high temperature and severe changes in metabolism. It is very rare, and the cause unclear, but it can be treated with large doses of a drug called dantrolene. Unfortunately, this facility didn't have enough dantrolene. This surgical facility did not have a bombproof procedure for dealing with malignant hyperthermia.

Although both of these procedures were cosmetic, these disasters could have happened with any type of surgery. So what do we learn?

To help evaluate the quality and safety of outpatient surgical centers, find out if the facility is licensed by your state or accredited by a national accrediting body such as the American Association for Accreditation of Ambulatory Surgical Facilities, the Joint Commission (formerly the Joint

Commission on Accreditation of Healthcare Organizations) or the Accreditation Association for Ambulatory Health Care. Any amount of outside vetting is better than none. Although these agencies are pretty malignant and picky, and I have been sorely tempted on more than one occasion to strangle these people, they do keep you honest. (Making me tuck my ponytail in is a bit extreme.) They are the ones that find out if you have a plan for everything.

Don't be fooled by glitz. Cosmetic surgery is filled with hucksters, and because it is a cash business, everyone and their Lhaso Apso wants in. Interestingly, I have no competition when it comes to pressure sores on the backside. Hmmm. Make sure your surgeon is board-certified, and certified in the field you need. Three separate surgical boards have certified me, but you don't want me doing your brain tumor, for instance. Don't be afraid to ask your surgeon about facility accreditation, board certification, results, complications, mad patients and secrets regarding personal animal magnetism.

Complications and death can occur with surgery. Fortunately, they are very rare, but patients need to help manage that risk. Check it out. If a doctor is defensive or evasive, find another. And it looks like they will be needing a replacement on "Oprah," so stay tuned.

Medical Meetings—What a Trip

A couple of times a year I attend national medical conferences to keep abreast of the latest developments in treatment, technology, and industry-driven propaganda. One of the great challenges is sorting out the preening academic liars, shameless self-promoters, and the occasional good doctor with a good idea. Like any job or profession, it is always intriguing to see what other people are doing in other markets.

This meeting was in Miami, which used to be in the United States. When I asked the concierge in the downtown hotel where I could walk to see the sights, he said "depends on what you are packing." Added to the fact that Miami was experiencing record cold temperatures, it was all business.

This was a facial cosmetic meeting put on by some big-time New York, LA, and Miami surgeons. These are some of the guys that do the celebrities, the rich, and the wannabe of the above. During several of the sessions there were live surgical cases being broadcast into the auditorium, and we could ask questions of the surgeons doing the cases. The video quality was amazing, and it is really a great way to see and evaluate procedures. It was also amazing to see how really ordinary most of these guys are surgically, and that they gain their exalted status through extraordinary marketing and publicity machines. I didn't see anything we don't do as well or better in Billings (and vastly cheaper).

Some interesting trends have developed. The "thread lifts", those so-called non-invasive face lifts done with threads under the cheeks, appear to be quite dead. The "short-scar" facelift is becoming more popular as people seek less down time. The weakening economy has increased the use of fillers for lines under the eyes, nasal folds, and lips. Botox continues to be strong. Facial lasering is starting to become more defined, as the wimpier lasers aren't either working or holding up. The more aggressive lasers, such as the carbon dioxide fractionated laser, have more redness and downtime but have good results. There are a million lasers on the market, many promising minimal downtime, but people don't like paying for minimal results either. Basically it turns out that you can't get something for nothing, which is a big surprise.

One new technology that looks like it might be legitimate is ultrasonic fat removal. This is focused fat destruction, done with high frequency ultrasound, which is done without incisions across the skin. It basically uses high frequency energy to explode fat, which the body then absorbs. Called UltraPulse, it has shown real promise in European trials, and I will keep you posted. Of course the machine will cost 150,000 smackers, like every other machine out there.

There sure weren't many Nip and Tuck surgeons there that I could see. The vast majority were middle aged or older, dumpy, paunchy, and bald. I am admittedly middle aged, bald, and dumpy, but not paunchy, which made me feel quite superior.

Between the wives and industry reps, there were enough over-sized breast implants that, if dropped on Afghanistan, would crush the Taliban.

I also pondered the wisdom of a New York socialite surgeon wearing a five thousand dollar Armani outfit and a hairpiece that looked like it took fourth place in the Westminster dog show.

I came away with a few ideas about refinements in eyelid surgery, a few new perspectives on shaping noses, and considerable relief that we had invested in the right laser. Most of all, I felt once again that Billings is offering some of the best care in the country. Whether it is cosmetic surgery, cancer care, heart disease, or most other fields, we are doing state of the art care in an environment that doesn't have many of the problems of bigger markets. I think the quality of life offered in Montana attracts a level of talent and quality of person that is greater than one would expect in a market of this size. As a resident of Billings and Montana, I have the confidence that no matter what the condition, our facilities and our bald, paunchy, middle-aged, and dumpy providers are as good as anyone else's. And at least from what I can tell, so are the hairpieces.

America's Top Doctor

The autumnal gray has become the palette of all our activities—dark in the morning going to work, dark on the way home, nearly dark in the second half of the freshman football games. I can see why bears do what they do—pork out and crash until it cheers up. My son toils in a desultory fashion on a 1000 word paper, the assigned topic "respect." I have told him that since, as a tribe of skinny geeks, our family will not bask in the glow of gridiron glory, we will attempt to write well. His occasional, surreptitious sneers are not particularly respectful. In the kitchen, my wife is watching her favorite show, "Law and Order: Spousal Disappearance", and taking copious notes. Where's my cave?

One bright spot burst through the gloom this week. I received a letter in the mail, with gold embossing, informing me that I had been named one of "America's Top Plastic Surgeons." I must confess that I have privately harbored such feelings, but how nice it was to get affirmation from the "Consumer's Research Council of America." As the pleasurable buzz of this approbation circulated, I wondered who had nominated me, or how that they ascertained my topness. We hadn't submitted any charts or outcome data, and confidentiality prevents us from sharing any patient information. My mother could have nominated me. She nominated me once for the Nobel Prize in Medicine, because I did a redo mitral valve replacement on one of her sorority sister's husbands, and I managed not to whack him. Anyway, who cares, I am one of "America's Top Plastic Surgeons." In the letter was a description of the various plaques and trophies one could choose to document the award. I like the "Bellagio Summit" so far, a gilt-edged crystal trophy with your name etched in calligraphy. Only $399.00 plus shipping.

My partner, Steve Grosso, and I were doing a bilateral breast reconstruction later that day, when I sort of casually mentioned that I had received the honor. "Really", he said. "By any chance were you listed in Who's Who also?" Well actually....
"Yeah, there's a different scam for every sucker doctor out there. I just pitch all that stuff when I get it." Professional jealousy is certainly unattractive, although I became a bit concerned when he retrieved his crumpled up "America's Top Plastic Surgeon" letter from the garbage and dumped it on my desk.

Everywhere you look, there are ads and billboards and commercials that trumpet "five stars" and "Top 100" and rated this and rated that when it comes to health care. I must disclose that I have posed in some of those ads, back in my cardiac surgery days, my hairier days. One thing I learned from those experiences was that you could make yourself look about anyway you wanted to. If you wanted your hospital to get paid more, you listed every little thing wrong with the patient and every big or little thing that happed to them after surgery. The hospital reimbursement was good, but then it looked like you had a high complication rate, and you were not ranked as one of America's Top Heart Hospitals. If you were a Top 100, then you didn't get very good reimbursement.

When you were named Top This or Top That or Five Star Super Plus, whatever organization named you that then offered to sell you a marketing package that ranged from ten to hundreds of thousands of dollars.

So what can "America's Top Plastic Surgeon" tell you about how to assess quality? I can tell you that I have worked in probably sixty hospitals in my career. I think both hospitals in Billings are good. Not perfect, and we are always working at getting better, but I would feel comfortable with a family member in either one. I have worked in places to which I would not send a dead goat. I know the two hospitals here in town are very competitive, which I think keeps them sharp, and both have aggressive quality improvement programs that never quit.

Actually, the "Roman Stonecast" looks nice too. It's only $299.00, and is stone with black brass. Very cool.

What about doctors, other than his Topness? I'll tell you what I do. I don't pay much attention to stars or ratings. I ask around. Any doctor is going to have a patient or two who is mad, so check multiple sources. Make sure they have done a residency in their field, and that they are board certified or eligible. It is okay to ask a doctor's office for patient references, as many patients are willing to do that. Ask your friends and family about their experience with a doctor, their bedside manner, and their results. One of my first plastic surgery patients in Billings was a breast reduction, and she just whipped up her shirt at work one day after surgery, and I was on my way. No billboard can do that. Another good resource is your primary care provider. They will refer you to someone skilled and effective, because a good referral is a positive reflection on them, and importantly, they don't want to listen to you whine.

It is starting to sink in that maybe this award could be bogus. Man, that "Ambassador Series", with the high gloss ebony finish with silver beveled edges, $325.00, would look good in my waiting room.

My mom, my wife, and my kids (depending on regulatory and funding conditions), though, still think I am "America's Top Plastic Surgeon." That's all I need.

Who Me, Vain?

"Am I being vain?"

From time to time I am asked this question by a patient after we have discussed a cosmetic procedure. It is a deceptively simple question, as it opens up a complex discussion of the nature of personal appearance, pride, and how others perceive us.

I have never had vanity issues, personally, being blessed with the chiseled yet still sensual face of an Adonis, thick leonine locks of blonde cascading around rippling deltoids and pectorals, those caressing a broad chest whose every respiration implies sexual threat. That may be a bit of an exaggeration. Okay, more precisely an outright lie. I am a middle-aged bald guy whose face looks like it served as a bicycle seat for a rhino during the Tour De France. Like being an NFL quarterback or a rock virtuoso, certain things in life ain't gonna happen, and for me physical beauty is about as likely to happen as dunking on LeBron James' head.

Vanity is described as excessive pride in one's appearance. So where does that start and end? Well, I shower every day for one thing. Does that mean I destroy my natural oils and scent with industrial chemicals? Yeah. I shave, keep what's left of my hair mercifully short, and dress in a way that seems professional and gives my patients some degree of confidence that I didn't sleep under a box last night. So far, nothing too crazy.

Let's go a step further. Let's say I watch what I eat to some degree and limit the amount of Blue Moon beer I guzzle. I walk four to five miles most nights, and play a little hoop. You can make the case that those behaviors are healthy, sure, but deep down I don't want to be perceived as some old soft asexual has-been. There is probably here an element of vanity creeping in, but I feel most personally comfortable rolling that way.

Okay, let's say you are a sixty year old trim, fit, active person in excellent health, aging "gracefully" if there is such a thing, who just happens to have enough extra skin under your chin to upholster a living room sectional. The other signs of age—the wrinkles, etc. don't seem to bother you, but this turkey wattle—.. So here comes the question "Am I being vain?"

What I find interesting is that often after something, like in this case, a neck lift, no one notices except the patient. Skillfully done, the scars can be concealed and the excess skin removed without altering the person's basic appearance. Remember the Great Rule of Life—everyone is thinking and looking at him or herself, not you. They are stressing about their own neck, not yours. Theirs is fatter and baggier anyway.

So is it vain to nip and tuck, get a little Botox or some fillers, do your hair, lose your gut, upgrade the wardrobe? Who cares? Either do, or don't do something because it makes you feel personally more comfortable or confident, regardless of what anyone else thinks. Don't fret the vanity issue, but at the same time, if I ever feel from a discussion with a patient that they are doing something to please anyone else, I encourage them not to do it. I had a conversation with a very athletic, slender young woman with very small breasts whose boyfriend had suggested breast augmentation. She was comfortable with her figure, but wanted to please him. My medical advice: Keep your breasts, replace him instead. I wish I had a supply of decent boyfriends in our office closet like we do implants. I would make a freaking fortune.

Confidence and personal security are sexy. They arise from a complex of personal decisions with which we are instinctively and intellectually comfortable. This is the genetic code of our personality; intensely unique, so broader cultural notions of things like vanity aren't worth worrying about. Worry about global warming, your mouthy kid, your failing dishwasher, and how big a yacht I'm going to buy when I do invent Boyfriend In A Box.

Chapter 10
Mission Trips

Foreign medical missions are both intensely satisfying and, in my mind, politically and morally confusing. I keep doing them, and keep not figuring out how I feel about them.

~~~~~~

Off to Cuernevaca

I returned about a week ago from a 10 day trip to Cuernavaca, Mexico with Smile Network, an organization that focuses on the repair of cleft lips and palates in underserved areas of the world. It was one of those "out of the comfort zone" experiences for someone like me, being mildly skeptical of medical "missions".

I wonder sometimes if these foreign operations aren't a subtle manifestation of American altruistic imperialism, a belief that we need to save the world, or that foreign governments don't fund their own cleft lip and palate programs because they know we will pick up the slack. When I explained these concerns to a veteran of 13 of these missions, Dr. Walt Peet, he listened patiently and said "Maybe that's true, but the kids don't know the politics, and we do it only for the kids. Focus on the kids."

It's not hard to get to Cuernavaca, a mountainous, gorgeous place with a year-round temperature of 75-80 degrees. That is, once you get through airport security. I must be on some list, because I am always getting screened. There is a short list of people in my life that I want running their hands all over my body, and a very short list of men I want doing that. And those rubber gloves conjure some unpleasant associations.... This airport procedure seems much to me like checking women for prostate cancer. Anyway.

Friday and Saturday were screening days, where Walt and I saw 70 or so kids with all manner of cleft lips, cleft palates, and deformed noses or bad scars from previous repairs. Our hosts, the University of Mexico at Cuernavaca, supplied translators (most all of the high school students there speak English). These missions are very tightly organized, and whether it was screening kids or operating, you are expected to move quickly and efficiently. Each child is assigned a priority score, and Sunday we designed an operating schedule for the week.

Monday though Friday we did 50 operations in two operating rooms. It was an exhilarating experience—cleft surgery is some of the most demanding, technical, and artistic surgery there is, and basically an opportunity like this is a surgeon's candy store. There were certainly long, physical, surgery days, but in the evening we would go upstairs to the wards to see the postop kids, and the reactions of the kids and their parents would totally fire us up for the next day. Some of the older kids with bad deformities of their lips and noses would look in the mirror at their new faces, as if seeing themselves for the first time, seeing themselves as they should be-- "yeah, that's finally me." It's always fascinated me how the arrangement of some skin and soft tissue can so drastically alter how one human perceives another. Correction of a facial deformity is life altering, and the privilege of doing so many kids in a week humbled even a cynic such as myself.

We had a great team of mostly Minnesota based anesthesiologists, nurses, medical records people, the Smile Network coordinators, and the Mexican University staff. Everyone came to work hard, with the expectation that the care delivered would be every bit as good as that in Minneapolis or the Mayo Clinic.

I think I would like to do it again. It was a long time to be gone, 10 days, with a young family, although my kids suggested

Siberia as the next destination. There are some cultural issues as well—for instance I place a high cultural value on toilet seats, which apparently is not a priority in Mexican hospital bathrooms, bring your own paper. And the mud huts we slept in, well OK, they weren't huts, it was actually a motel; OK it was more like a resort, so it WAS a resort with two swimming pools, but nowhere in the Bible does it say you can't be comfortable doing the Lord's work.

Friday afternoon, as we were packing up the OR, the Mexican nurses, who had donated their week to assist us, put up a sign saying "God will bless you for what you have done." I think that is true, but not because we did surgery (for surgeons do that as ducks swim upon the water) but because we understand a little better that service to others may be the only really meaningful thing we do in our lives. In the bewildering intellectual miasma that is human experience, the touch of one hand on another may be all the understanding we need.

Mountain Magic

Some guys call you up and invite you to go on seedy sports junkets, insalubrious fishing expeditions, or the putative "golf" outing. I think my wife longs at times that I had such disreputable pals, because my friend Walt Peet calls with schemes involving an extended week of surgery in southern Mexico. "Like a candy store, man, all the cleft lips and palates you can do." This trip, to Tuxtla, Gutierrez, in the Mexican state of Chiapas, was put together by Smile Network, a smaller, tight organization out of Minneapolis that works closely with local medical officials in areas that need help with meeting demand for repairing cleft lip and palate malformations.

I collected another deadbeat Billings, MT husband and father, anesthesiologist Chuck Aragon, and twelve hours later and multiple body cavity searches later (Chuck looks a terrorist from central casting) we made it to Tuxtla. The day before surgery we toured a small town high in the mountains called San Juan Chamula. Naturally, since we were way south in Mexico, it was snowing, and from a street side vendor I bought a coat that looked like a recently eviscerated sheep that had not recently bathed. Our mission pediatrician, gourmand, and tour guide Assidro took us to San Sebastian, a centuries old church, where the residents practice a numinous fusion of Catholicism and traditional Mayan beliefs. The interior of the cavernous cathedral was illuminated by thousands of votive candles, clusters of them burning in front of effigies of saints, all of them European white guys. One wizened woman kneeling on the floor was holding a live chicken, passing it gently over the flickering candles, as if in a sanctifying ritual. We watched mesmerized, our interest intensifying when she snapped the chicken's neck. The thin gray smoke from the candles wafted to the capacious ceiling, as if in communion with the offerings from centuries earlier.

As in prior missions we saw cute babies with wide clefts, and then (perhaps vainly) basked in the approbation of the grateful parents when they saw their child repaired, their child now as they had expected, for no parent expects their baby's face to be rent asunder. In some Mexican dialects the term for cleft deformities translates as "cursed." But this trip I was struck by the teenagers we saw, the awkward adolescents whose life had been dominated by the stigma of a lip in a perpetual sneer, or a twisted and misshapen nose. Their downcast countenance, their every body syllable designed to minimize the observer's view of the deformity, each signal they emitted spoke of a crushingly low self esteem. I was (and arguably, still essentially am) a skinny, pimply geeky teenager, and no amount of cover-up, hair gel, or barbells could mitigate the disaster that was me. But oh my, I can't begin to get a grip on what these kids have lived with. Edgar is seventeen, and just seemed whipped by the way he looked. After surgery, his father, bursting with pride, said "finally Edgar is worthy to carry on our family name." We didn't know whether to be pleased or completely creeped out.

Cleft surgery is a jambalaya of chess, a Rubrik's cube, and a thousand piece puzzle. Look at your own lip in the mirror. Your nostrils are separated by the columella down the middle. The groove from the base of the columella down to the lip is called the philtral column, and then that blends into your upper lip, which has the little Cupid's bow in the middle, and the delicate white roll along the edge of the lip. The red part of the lip is the vermillion, which gives fullness to the lip. In the space of a half inch in a cleft lip baby, every one of these lines and bumps and dips and doodles is screwed up, even the muscles and skin inside the lip. Imagine a symphonic orchestra, with a hundred instruments. For the sound to be beautiful, each instrument is delicately and precisely balanced against each other, and each has to be consonant with the other. We may not know anything about music, but we know when it is right. A lip is similar—you may know nothing of anatomy but you know if a lip is right.

I think our team had a symphonic resonance as well. Thousands of miles away from home, I felt the easy comfort of an operating room staffed by experienced pros, recovery and ward nurses who just handled stuff, and records and support staff who pushed the ball up the floor. We had two surgical crews in adjacent rooms, and I am quite convinced that Walt and Chuck's music came from Wifebeatertunes.com. Other than a little subliminal competition over who had the largest admiring posse in the OR at a given time, thing were reasonably congenial. Our accommodations were simple, the usual straw mat on the dirt floor of a thatched hut. Okay, that's a lie. But the room service was *slow*.

Standing in San Sebastian, the faintly foreboding images of the Saints ephemeral in the candlelight, I wondered if we were just a contemporary manifestation of a Eurocentric theological/medical road trip. But in the rafters, in that vast space above the altar, I saw not cardinals in robes but the spirits of hard working monks and priests who were ignorant ot geopolitics. They lived and died in poverty and obscurity in a remote village so that people there would know that God loves them. I let the political considerations, like the smoke from the candles, rise and dissipate. I hope that a teenager with a bad lip and nose, or the family of a baby with a hole in its face, knows that someone loves them.

A Smile Uncovered

I saw her across a crowded lobby and knew I must meet her. The telltale signs were all there—a hand always across the

114

mouth and upper lip, sometimes a bandana, even a mask. A willowy girl of thirteen with smiling eyes, mocha brown against amber skin.

I skipped across the lobby of the Hospital para el Nino Poblano in Puebla, Mexico, and dragging an interpreter, introduced myself to Maricela.

The left side of her nose was wide and slumped with a jagged scar at its base. Her upper lip was deeply notched with a typical "harelip" configuration. My hands began to sweat. I looked nervously around. So far Walt Peet, my surgical partner on this trip, hadn't seen her. Like any top-level surgeon, he would want to do the most challenging cases.

This wasn't a good time for a surgical mission. The end of the year is when everyone is trying to get that elective operation done if they have met their insurance deductible for the year. We are opening a new building in two weeks, my son's football team was playing for a state championship, and I am gallivanting in a country better known for shootouts with high body counts than medical sophistication.

Frankly I have some reservations about the whole concept of "missions" in general. Some of these countries seem to have plenty of money for everything but taking care of their indigent or native peoples. My compadres in these ventures tell me that thinking too much about these things is not good, especially when you are not that bright to start with. Shut up and operate.

I don't have any idea what my life would be like if I had been born looking like someone had taken an axe to the middle of my face. I certainly know I don't have the strength of character to have the delightfully sunny disposition that Maricela has. I have had every conceivable advantage in life—white, male, great parents, super education, health—and here looking at me was a slip of a girl with more guts than I will ever have.

In that frenetic lobby, I think I finally got the point. All these people—nurses, anesthesiologists, pediatricians, OR techs, medical records personnel, dozens of Mexican student volunteers, this whole army of good souls—were here to honor someone who can find joy in even the most challenging of existences, to say "hey girl, we think you are pretty special, and why don't we fix that lip and nose."

Next to our hotel in Puebla is a beautiful four hundred year old church with fabulous sacred art and statues. Sitting alone in the deep granite silence, the souls of long passed healers sharing my contemplative ruminations, I studied the images of saints, especially their lips and noses. I thought of those artists of antiquity, exquisitely rendering images of the divine, their work also their worship.

During Maricela's operation, I felt the gentle but critical counsel of those artists hovering over me—"make that nasal sill just a bit narrower, her lip must be fuller, it must be perfect. You cannot honor God with anything less than your best."

I was so anxious to see her reaction after surgery, to give her a mirror so she could see herself in a way that did not require a concealing hand or mask. Her smile was beatific—but no more than before her surgery. Although she was delighted, her smile emanated from a place that knows no lips or noses or flesh.

We learn so much from the unanticipated, the things we don't think about but rather happen unbidden. The artists of the Puebla cathedral were never aware of my existence, but inspired me nonetheless. Whether our job is to stack boxes in a warehouse, take out a linebacker, or repair lips and noses, giving our best is how we state whom we are, and how we demonstrate our worthiness for the gifts we were given.

Sometimes a smile will challenge and teach and chastise all at once. A smile uncovered, revealed, can be all the motivation we require.

Completing the Circle

Our recent trip with Smile Network to Puebla, Mexico, to do cleft lip surgery was scheduled for Thursday, March 8.

In February the trip was back on, then off, back on in March, then for double dog sure cancelled the Wednesday before we were supposed to leave. I cancelled the flights for my son and daughter, and began scheduling the next week in my office.

As I was walking out of the surgery center that afternoon, our team leader, Dr. Chuck Aragon, said, "wait a minute, there's been a breakthrough, and we're going."

With all the uncertainty, we'd figure we'd evaluate maybe 40 kids there and operate on 30. So of course we ended up seeing 140 kids, operating on 62 lips and palates.

Our most joyous moments are the least expected. Since the mission had appeared to be limited, part of our crew was left home. Thus my 17-year-old son Luke and Chuck's 19-year-old daughter Alexa took on increased roles. A very artful instructor, Vicki, turned them into a seven case a day powerhouse. My daughter Sally served as a recovery nurse, which was also cool except for her belief that, regardless of the setting, you can talk back to Dad.

At one point in the 80-degree sauna that was the OR, I thought "in five years I won't be able to do this." Then, across the hall, I see Dr. Walt Peet, *fifteen years my senior*, cranking out one beautiful baby after another, and I had to man up.

At the end of a long day, Chuck, came in the OR talking about an 18 year-old girl who had never been out of the house or gone to school because her father was embarrassed by her "monstrous" appearance. When the father left town, her brother snuck over and brought her to us.

The girl wore a mask, and obviously was very socially delayed. A cleft lip in an adult is even more startling than that of a baby.

During the operation, our crew hustled out and bought a mirror for the girl, which we all signed. Postop, she and her brother looked in the mirror at an appealing, almost striking young woman. A joyous moment for us was for her, I think, one of shock. Imagine looking in the mirror and seeing someone new.

Of all life experiences, the communion of a team to accomplish a goal has to be among the greatest. I would go to the holding area and take these precious little eight pound peanuts from their mothers, and carry them, their wispy soft breath on my neck, to the operating room. There, a rhythm of IV tubes and breathing tubes and cutting and sewing and moving and shaping commenced—hands and minds and spirit in concert to make the most beautiful of music. Each team member added their touch to this little soul—from the OR to recovery to the nursing ward—and then the circle was complete, back to their mother and their life ahead.

Chapter 11
The Heart of Christmas

Christmas memories are often among our most intense. A health crisis or tragedy can be particularly wounding or poignant during and long after the holidays. These stories are a big part of my Christmas history. The New Year resolution pieces are just plain silly.

~~~~~~~~~~~~~~~~~~~~~~~~~~~~~~

Rudolf the Red Nosed Plaintiff

The condition characterized by a large, porous, bulbous, and red nose is known as rhinophyma. Rhinophyma is thought to be a type of rosacea. Rosacea is a common condition characterized by symptoms of facial flushing and a spectrum of clinical signs, including redness, spidery veins, coarseness of skin, and an in eruption resembling acne. Rhinophyma means a big, red, lumpy sort of nose that can be most distressing to the owner.

Before discussing the medical and surgical treatment of rosacea, I feel I must comment on the dirty little secret that is Rudolf the Red Nosed Reindeer. As you know, Rudolf the Red Nosed Reindeer had a very shiny nose. All of the other reindeer, presumably Dasher and Dancer and their homies, used to laugh and call him names. They never let poor Rudolf join in any reindeer games. Those facts are public record.

This reflects an extremely insensitive and intolerant attitude on the part of the supposedly sweet and cute reindeer that deliver presents to our children. Apart from being morally repugnant, does the ostracizing of a member of a particular constituency on the basis of a physical feature not constitute a violation of the Americans with Disabilities Act (ADA)? Santa's lawyers, themselves all very short guys with pointed ears, point out that the North Pole is not under American jurisdiction, but the Justice Department has countered by saying that since Santa delivers toys in the United States, he is obligated to comply. So far, the incoming Obama administration has taken no position on the issue, as they are still unsure whether Santa was involved in the Illinois Senate situation.

And where was Santa in all this? What did he know and when did he know it? Certainly the fact that Rudolf was continually harassed, so much that someone wrote a song about it, indicates a pattern of systemic abuse. So either Santa knew about it and looked the other way, or is this a Santa who is simply out of touch? Either scenario is chilling.

Then one foggy Christmas Eve, Santa came to say "Rudolf with your nose so bright, won't you guide my sleigh tonight?" Now all of a sudden Rudolf is useful. Maybe Santa was seeing two sleighs, or they don't call him Blitzen for nothing, but I suspect there was a big settlement that night, because now all the reindeer love him. But do they love Rudolf, really, or just suck up to him because Santa has thrown the big red furry arm of endorsement around him? Remember, this guy is coming down your chimney. You can bet that whenever some TV preacher gets caught in an overly intensive counseling session with a stripper that it will be all over CNN, but Santa allows frat house style hazing and gets a pass. Go figure. Anyway, I just wanted to get that off my chest.

The causes of rosacea, and rhinophyma, the nasal manifestation, are unknown. Speculation has centered around abnormalities in the dermis, such that normal fluids and bacteria are not normally cleared away. There is excessive dilation of blood vessels. Certain types of bacteria are found in excess

120

in rhinophyma. It may be that exposure to harsh climates, actinic radiation (too much sun), or exposure to chemicals, spicy foods, and alcohol have a role. There is a stereotypical association of a big red nose and alcoholism that has only a partial basis in fact.

Rhinophyma can be treated with topical retinoids such as Retin-A, which help with the turnover of abnormal cells. Antibiotics such as tetracycline are sometimes useful. For very bulbous noses, surgical therapy such as laser ablation or direct excision can significantly improve the shape and appearance of the nose. These treatments are helpful but not curative.

Rosacea, and its nasal component rhinophyma, can be distressing and uncomfortable conditions. If you have unusual redness or porosity on your face, and are developing a lot of spider veins on the face or nose, you should consult your provider to make sure of the diagnosis and to rule out more serious conditions.

I have nothing against Santa, really. I'm sure it was just a mistake that every time I wrote him a letter and asked for a G.I. Joe action figure he sent me a Ken Doll. Real funny. Just wait until he asks me for some liposuction.

Teach Your Children Well (Or Better Than Me)

A few days before Christmas in 1990, in St. Louis, Missouri, our young family was foggy with fatigue. I was in the last year of an eight-year surgical residency, we had a five-month-old baby, and our 18 month old had long since discarded napping. Our plan on this dreary, soggy Saturday was for my older daughter and I to get baby Cathy down for a nap, the two of us to go out and kick around, and allow mom to get a desperately needed rest.

Sally and I began singing one of our stock lullabies

> Tiny baby, go to sleep
> Slumber gently, slumber deep

Cathy, a rather rotund baby resembling a Bears middle linebacker, not even a little bit sleepy, finally feigned sleep so we would shut up.

We went to the car wash, an activity designed to consume time and entertain a toddler. My enormous, prehistoric cell phone shrilled. My junior resident on the pediatric cardiac surgery service at St. Louis Children's Hospital sounded as if was being chased by one of the local crack dealers.

"Man, you gotta come. A little girl got her chest crushed when her dad backed a car out of the garage, and they can't keep her alive on the respirator. They want to put her on ECMO *right now* and I don't know how to do that. You gotta come *now*!"

ECMO stands for extracorporeal membrane oxygenation, which means basically that you put someone on a heart lung machine to support their lungs and circulation in the hopes that the crushed lungs will recover in a few days. In a child that means putting tubes in the carotid artery and jugular vein in the neck, and connecting them to the heart lung machine. These are small vessels in a child, in this case a 3 year old, and the procedure is done in a great hurry.

There was no time to take Sally home. I tucked her under my arm, her pink Osh Kosh bibs soaked, and raced for the pediatric intensive care unit.

The unit was a frenzy of activity—the perfusionists setting up the machine, the ICU doctors desperately trying to ventilate the child, a nurse trying to console the devastated parents. I plopped Sally on a stool right next to the bed and said "do not move; you don't leave that stool or Santa won't come."

I sliced open the little girl's neck, thankfully cannulated the vessels without a problem, and shortly her blue lips turned pink. It would be days, weeks, months before we would know if that little girl was going to be OK, but for now the crisis was averted.

I turned to the stool. No Sally. I searched the room, the whole PICU, no luck. No one had seen her, and of course I freaked. I went up and down the halls, the stairs, checked the elevator. Finally I looked in the newborn ICU, which was adjacent to the PICU, and saw a flash of pink bottom.

She had climbed up on another stool, and somehow opened the door to an isolette, a little plastic house for a premature baby. This little two-pound prune was on a respirator, and had been moving around uncomfortably. Sally reached in with her 18 month old little finger, and was stroking the cheek of this tiny person struggling to stay alive.

> *Eyenee beebee, go to ah sweep*
> *Sumber genly, sumber deep*

I didn't know which I would be charged with—child neglect or endangering a premature baby, so I grabbed her and ran. Fortunately all the activity kept us from being caught.

On the way home I explained to my daughter that Mommy didn't need to know any of this, especially about her being lost, because Mommy was tired, and sometimes it is better not to upset people unnecessarily. Co-opting a child into a cover-up would be another way of stating this, and for those parents who have never colluded with a child in a prevarication of sorts, go have an extra tofu after your yoga class.

When we got home, the baby was bouncing, and Mommy was coming slowly back to consciousness. "What did you two do?" she asked Sally.

"We washed the car and daddy cut the baby."

"That's nice."

Twenty years later Sally, now a senior in nursing school, and I went to Mexico with Smile Network to do a week of cleft lip and palate surgery. She worked in the OR and recovery and on the floor, growing into her role while daddy cut the babies.

Our children pay little heed to our sermons, but do watch closely what we do. My mother was a pharmacist and I learned to hang out in hospitals. Many of our career and business influences are family. Whether we lay block or fall trees or cut babies, if we do it with pride and a good effort, our children will feel that, while tuning out what they hear.

At Christmas, I think of the Christ child, maybe perched on a stool, learning to be a carpenter in Joseph's shop. Some day he would become the Messiah, but first he had to learn to work hard, to care about his craft, and most importantly, how to teach.

The Open Heart

It was one of those intensely dark, deep December nights, at least a decade ago, back in my heart surgery days, when we went to my wife's "Ladies Night Out" Christmas party.   The location, a block from the hospital, was most convenient for my on-call status, but said status left me somewhat resentful and abstemious among the other spouses. I could certainly eat, however, but just before dinner the ER called. Some guy, only blocks away, had been stabbed in the chest in some chemically fueled conflict, and was on his way in with barely detectable vital signs.

He and I arrived at the same time. His breathing was agonal, which is that of a dying person resembling a fish out of water. No longer responsive and his face blue, he was quickly intubated by the ER physician to secure the airway. Blood pressure was unobtainable, and his heart rate was now 160. Drifting through the corner of my vision, I briefly thought I saw Tami MacDonald, one of the cardiac surgery charge nurses.

The guy's only hope was to get him to the OR immediately and relieve what appeared to be cardiac tamponade, which is when a hole in the heart leads to bleeding in the sac around the heart. The heart is compressed by the blood around it, and can't fill or squeeze. That option evaporated when the distressed heart fibrillated, going from a wildly contracting muscle to a quivering and ineffectual organ in the chest of a man now dead.

124

We washed his chest in betadine, an antiseptic, as it became apparent we would have to open him there in the ER. I took off my new Christmas sweater, a rich emerald and black, so it wouldn't be ruined in the coming tumult. I put on a blue paper gown, despairing that I would have to try to cut between the ribs to get to the heart, because I had none of my regular tools.

I'd often wondered how those shepherds felt, on the first Christmas, keeping watch over their flocks by night, when suddenly an angel of the Lord appeared in the sky. Whoa. Now I know, because as I reluctantly picked up the scalpel, Tami appeared with Kathy Kennedy, one of my cardiac scrub technicians, and they had brought all my toys from the OR—a sternal saw, a retractor, every present you can put under the tree. One vertical slice to the bone, a quick run up the sternum with the saw, open up the pericardium with the Mayo scissors, and we were there.

His heart, blue and distended, undulated weakly but defiantly as it died. There was a short, clean rent in the right ventricle where the knife had entered, and black, desaturated blood oozed. Kathy gave me just the stitch I wanted, a 3-0 Prolene on an SH needle, a bright blue, Christmas ornament-looking stitch with a white felt pledget on the thread so it wouldn't pull through the almost gelatinous heart muscle.

One stitch closed the hole. The heart was repaired but not beating, and I thought desperately *if only I had internal defibrillator paddles,* which Tami promptly produced in another miracle. One shock and that moribund heart leapt joyously back to life.

The heart blasted liters of blood to the oxygen-starved brain, which then snapped out of it and ordered a round of breathing. The man's large chest then violently contracted, and all the blood pooled in his chest from the stab wound was expelled in a mighty gush into my face and onto my paper gown, which promptly dissolved. Soaked in blood and now bare chested, I watched in horror as he then sat bolt upright, his heart swinging wildly out of his chest, and I mused that things were getting a little weird. The alert ER physician quickly anesthetized the guy, and we scooted up to the OR and washed him out and closed him.

Afterward, I stood in the shower in the OR locker room, the hot water loosening the clotted blood from my body hair and sworling crimson around the drain, and I reflected on what had happened. All those people in the ER, my trusty OR crew with whom I have shared thousands of cases, the people in central processing who get all the tools together and clean, everyone at that moment in time came together, read the situation perfectly, and had executed the ultimate two minute drill. I went back to the ER, found my new sweater tucked gently in a corner, and went back to the party.

Two days later, it was like nothing had ever happened to the guy. He was fine. I sat at his bedside, preparing him for discharge, and told him that a lot of people had done an incredible job to save him, that I felt his survival was as close to miraculous as it could be. "Whatever," he said, "that's a nice story but let's make sure I get plenty of Percocet, okay?" I just lost it at that point, and unleashed a thoroughly unprofessional sermon right from the fourth chapter of the Gospel of Dirty Harry: "Listen, punk, you're just another piece of garbage I stepped in while I was on call. You're like the sixth idiot I've fixed with a stab to the heart, and the first five were just as useless as you." I stomped out, discharged him, and wrote a prescription for ibuprofen. You and your posse party down on that.

Eight months later, I was chilling in my office when some guy strode in, walked right by reception and up to my desk. He emphatically slapped down two pieces of paper in front of me and delivered a challenging glare. One of the documents was a culinary certificate from a local technology college, and the other was a pay stub from a restaurant. He then delivered on sentence, each word laden with fervor "I ...am not....a piece... of garbage." He then dramatically exposed his now healed sternotomy scar.

When the night is cold and dark and deep, and it seems that our lives are predictable and even grinding at times, there always

126

exists the possibility that a bright light, even a star, will appear and change everything. Christmas is ultimately about a light in the darkness, the belief that redemption is always possible. It is also a challenge to each of us to live our lives, as seemingly as ordinary as they are, with an attitude of excellence, so that when the moment arrives that we transform the mundane into magic, we might hear the angels sing.

The Gift

My Christmas Eve story dates back to 1987, when I was a surgical resident on the cardiac surgery service at the University of Utah. A few days earlier, we had admitted Mack Brown, a 45-year-old man with severe congestive heart failure. His weakened and dilated heart was beyond repair, and his sallow complexion, fluid distended abdomen, grossly swollen legs, and labored breathing were the hallmarks of a person more dead than alive. A widower, his only family was his 13 year old daughter, Madeline, a preternaturally composed girl whose childhood was truncated not only by the loss of her mother but the impending specter of further unbearable hurt. Our plan was to keep Mack alive long enough to receive a heart transplant.

So it was Christmas Eve, the afternoon light waning quickly in the snowy Salt Lake winter, when the organ transplant service contacted the University, saying that there was a heart available in eastern Colorado. This potentially exciting news was tempered by the information that the donor, a 17-year-old boy, shot in the head with a bullet meant for another, had been "down" for an unknown period of time, and it was unclear how much damage could have been done to the heart from a lack of oxygen. The echocardiogram looked OK but not great. The transplant staff had a discussion with Mack and Madeline, and everyone agreed that with Mack's poor status that we would accept the heart.

The distance from Salt Lake to the town where the donor was located was fairly great, and hearts are best transplanted when they have been stopped for four hours or less. That meant we had to really move. This required a "high performance aircraft", and the Mrs. Field's Cookies people agreed to let us use their very fast corporate jet. As one of the junior but not entirely useless members of the transplant service, I was elected to fly to Colorado to retrieve the donor heart. The big boys would open up Mack, remove his weary heart, and prepare him to receive the new one.

I flew to the Salt Lake Airport on a helicopter with Bill, the cardiovascular PA assigned to assist me. There we beheld the Mrs. Field's jet, a gorgeous red and gold 12 passenger Gulfstream. Red leather seats, a full (and alas, untouched) bar, and a general glow of utter civility were disturbed only by the irony of our red and white Playmate cooler sitting on the lush carpet. The wonderfully complex miracle that is the human heart is transported in a sterile plastic sack in a fifteen-dollar plastic box meant for Bud Lite.

After a "high performance takeoff" we were soon at 30,000 feet, hurtling through the now darkness of Christmas Eve, the air outside at minus 50 degrees Fahrenheit, the moon improbably below us. Bill, a rather sardonic soul, mused "Consider this: here we are, flying through the night on Christmas Eve, bringing this man and his daughter what they want more than anything in the world, in a red and gold cookie jet. Subtract a couple of Pratt and Whitney engines, add a few reindeer, and we're there."

At the small community hospital, we arrived just as the donor was being taken to the operating room. A matronly black woman, presumably his mother, was stroking his face and speaking softly to him. His vacant eyes, the windows of a lifeless brain, were surrounding by the grotesque swelling and purple discoloration of the lethal head injury.

In the operating room were three other surgeons—two from Pittsburg for the liver, and a guy from Wisconsin after the kidneys. All were foreign transplant fellows, all from the Middle or Far East, their musical accents floating above the ambient noise of the OR. Bill and I looked at their coolers lined up against the wall, again all Playmates, and we speculated on which had the incense and which the myrrh.

We opened the chest with an electric saw, then attached a tube to the aorta, just above the heart, and infused very cold saline into the cardiac vessels to make it stop. I then took a pair of heavy scissors and cut that boy's heart out of his chest. I did this many times in my former life as a heart surgeon, but I never got over how utterly macabre that act was. I wrapped the heart in a bag of sterile saline solution, and laid it in the cooler.

When we arrived back at the hospital in Salt Lake City, I saw Madeline waiting outside the OR. She saw the cooler, her father's life in a picnic bucket, and asked in a voice ever so soft yet unwavering "Is it good?" Stunned by her fortitude, I could only croak "Madeline, it is a good heart."

The big boy surgeons sewed that heart in with the casual elegance of the truly self-possessed. When Mack's warm blood surged down the heart's arteries, the sleeping organ leapt to the task and resumed a robust rhythm, eschewing the usual defibrillation required.

After surgery, I stopped by the ICU stall where Mack was recovering. There were nurses, respiratory therapists, and laboratory technicians gathered around the bed. At the head was Madeline, the tips of her fingers touching her father's face, a face now rosy in the glow of abundant perfusion. Her expression was not the besieged anxiety of the frantic relative, but rather the beatific confidence of one whose knowledge surpasses understanding.

I stepped out into the dazzling blue and white wonder that was Christmas day along the Wasatch front. I thought about how little I really knew about giving. I thought about a mother in Colorado, who gave her son so that the little family that was Madeline and her daddy would have new life. I thought about a young mother, two thousand years ago, who knew that she would see her son, who would be the Christ, die for others as well. I hope I never have to make that type of gift, to give more than I can bear. What I must give is my best, to share and multiply and be worthy of what others have given to me.

A Black and Decker Christmas

How can a Black and Decker Workmate Bench stir such powerful emotions?

Some of my most indelible Christmas memories are those of returning home to Missoula from college or medical school. Finals weeks in pre-med or medical school are frankly awful. A couple of weeks of cramming and then a week of comprehensive exams in calculus, physics, biology, chemistry, and any other semi-elective horrors is bad enough, but add to that the knowledge that if you don't get A grades in most if not all of them, you are not going to The Show. What a cocktail of stress, caffeine, insomnia, poisonous calories, and finally, frank hallucinations.

My brother, also a physician, was only a couple of years behind me, and so we shared the muzzy fog that hung over our post-nuclear psychological state. Unable to sleep, we sat in front of the Christmas tree, staring mutely at the colored lights, pondering which of them represented the correct answer.

When dawn arrived, we ventured out Christmas shopping. We'd walk to the mall, having the vestigial sense not to drive, and make our first stop.

This was the bar. Realize, in my lame defense, that the drinking age in Montana back then was 18. This does not excuse ordering a gin and tonic when offered the breakfast menu, but my biological time zone at that point was in Berzerkistan.

After an indeterminate period of time at breakfast, we resolved to acquire gifts for our family members. Of course, we didn't do that, but wandered blearily through the gaily-decorated stores looking like we might pull AR-15s out of our jackets and make national news.

130

Dads are especially hard guys for whom to shop. I am a dad, and the only thing I want costs 1,250,000 dollars. I have everything else or don't want or need it. Our dad, a build-it kind of guy, had all the tools, books, ties, and other stuff we had desperately hacked up in previous sodden trips to the mall.

I had it in my head that he needed a Black and Decker Workmate Bench. This was a combination vice and sawhorse kind of thing, which was purportedly portable. Perfect.

Wrong, said my brother. We would stand in Sears and look at the thing, and he would pillory the idea with the coruscating contempt. "This thing is for lightweights, guys without a real vice, or a real sawhorse, the sparkling wine crowd, the poseurs, the '19.95, but wait, there's more' crowd." To him, the Black and Decker Workmate Bench represented tool belt bourgeois, man pretending to be Real Man. We'd quarrel irresolutely, me wondering if he was in fact talking about me instead of the bench, and then wander back to the bar.

Probably six Christmases of this, and we never bought the bench.

I saw one of the silly things this week. Dad's been gone over two years now, a wonderful, sweet, gentle man. A guy who supported his wife's professional career in the late 1940s. A devout but never censorious man who asked us "How's your soul today?"

I've learned a lot from that loss. He was 87, but I never say "Oh, it's OK, he was 87. It's never OK, is it?

I've learned that holidays intensify feelings of loss.

Years ago I got a lady, about 62, from Cody with a huge inferior myocardial infarction on Christmas Eve. I spent all night operating on her, coaxing her off the pump, and all Christmas Day trying to keep her alive. The patient's only surviving relative, a daughter, was there at the beside as we clipped the treetops. All I could think of was "I can't let this lady's mom die on Christmas." There was a little plastic Christmas tree in that

ICU room, and I remember looking at the lights, in the middle of the night, and thinking "man, I've been here before."

This is an emotionally charged time of year, time for you to do some doctoring, to reach out to someone who's had a loss. If you've had a loss, wrap your arms around it and squeeze it, because the ache represents something wonderful you once had. As surely as we had the manger, we also had the cross.

Someday, when my brother's time on earth has ended, and he crosses the Elysian Fields, he will experience a moment of both great joy and great humility. For he will see our father, again young and strong, working on a piece of wood-- firmly in the grip of a Black and Decker Workmate Bench.

What Not To Do In The New Year

I don't know how many articles I've read over the last couple of weeks regarding advice for improving health in the New Year. They all say the same things, and all are boring and exceedingly pious in tone. I believe that there is a secret plot, promulgated by the CIA, the Trilateral Commission, and the vast Ambidextrous Conspiracy to keep us from enjoying ourselves. As one of your Health Section voices of truth amidst the cacophony of whole-wheat-rabbit-food-eating Birkenstock propaganda, I will enlighten you regarding the great myths of health maintenance. Let's go down the list.

Quit smoking. Ever hear that one? A recent study from Atlanta showed that ER visits for heart attack dropped 40% when an indoor smoking ban was passed for bars and restaurants. Remarkably, the very first study of that kind was done in Helena, MT, with similar results. So? One of the keystones of the Billings area economy is health care. Cardiovascular disease and cancer care are two of the three major product lines for both St. Vincent Healthcare and Billings Clinic. The last thing we need from a regional economic standpoint is a big drop in cancer and heart disease. Many of my homeboys are cardiovascular and cancer doctors. They have expensive toys and exotic supermodel spouses. Do **you** want to be responsible for them having to drive a Honda instead of a BMW? The horror. Frankly it would be unpatriotic for you to quit smoking. In times like this, everyone has to do his or her part. President-Elect Obama was bullied into smoking cessation, but others must stand firm. The British National Health Service calculated that smokers actually had lower health care costs over a lifetime than non-smokers, meaning that smokers actually helped their country. By dying young, actually, but that is beside the point.

Lose weight (yawn). Another tired pearl of drivel. It is only common sense that a skinny person is far more likely to get run over crossing the street than a bigger person. You can't see the string beans. Also, a wiry vegan will do a whole lot less damage to the front end of your F-150 than your basic offensive tackle, so you are less likely to swerve to miss them. Being inadequately padded will harm your love life, as no one wants to get too close to a lot of sharp edges. Sixty per cent of your brain is fatty acids, which might explain why the lettuce and tofu crowd is so dull. The list is endless.

Exercise more. Several of my colleagues are these ropy, jackrabbit types who ride their bikes hundreds of miles a month. They have resting heart rates of 45, body fat of 8%, and cholesterols well below their I.Q. They will live forever, but... not so fast. In the last few years there have been multiple rib fractures, a pneumothorax, a fractured pelvis, broken legs, wrists, a crushed trachea, etc. These guys have racked up more health care spending that Dick Cheney. So use a treadmill, you say? Remember the cartoon the Jetsons, where George got pancaked? I don't think so. I have yet to get injured watching football on TV, unless you count that time I got tangled up in the beer tap and cracked my head on the subwoofer. Exercise is dangerous and wears you out besides. No one every tore an ACL changing the channel.

Eat right. I read this thing where you are supposed to "eat the rainbow". Different colored foods, such as lettuce, red peppers, blue berries, etc. are supposed to give you fiber and antioxidants and vitamins and all that stuff. I guess I would have to agree with some of that. Both Skittles and peanut M&Ms come in all those colors, and I try to cover the spectrum.

This thing with cholesterol has to be individualized. The central molecule of most hormones is cholesterol, and low cholesterol is fine for you hybrid driving metros who use a lot of skin care products, but those of us with fairly massive testosterone outputs need at least two cheeseburgers a day to stay flush. I am not opposed to new thinking in nutrition, as I am looking forward to the introduction of the Organic Hostess Ding Dong.

Remember the most important thing you can do for your health—get people in your life. It is our connection to others that enriches and sustains us. Relationships are either built-in (family), or intentional (everything else). It's hard when you are tired, or have worked all day to go to meetings, groups, church, volunteer jobs, games, theater, or classes. We are becoming a society of cocoons, home in front of a screen of some sort, while our civic organizations and civility in general dwindle. Isolation is definitely not healthy, and without mental health we cannot enjoy physical health. People and relationships don't happen, they are hard work and can be disappointing and frustrating at times. There are, however, those evanescent joys of connection, those delectable reinforcements of our humanity, that Skittles and beer in front of the TV cannot match.

I Resolve To......Maybe Next Year

One of my New Year's resolutions is definitely not resolving to be on time, thus the appearance of this missive clearly too late for the really new year. That would also mean I would have to stay on time in my office, which is unlikely, because my favorite part of medicine is talking to my patients, sometimes about fairly off the wall stuff (what magical realism in Central American literature has to do with breast reconstruction isn't always clear.) Since I'm already late getting to the point, which is Health Resolutions for the New Year, I can't claim time efficiency as a goal.

Let's start with eating worse, not better. I'm sure you are as tired as I am of all the yapping about eating healthy. I'm not a bad cook, actually, if I can use butter, cream, salt, and a lot of wine—some of which actually gets into the recipes. I like to make elaborate gravies in large quantities, so that there is enough for leftovers. Having to use a chainsaw the next day to get the gravy out of the storage container tells me the fat content may be a bit high. Eating better means highly viscous oozy gravy on a rib eye. Eating worse means steamed broccoli on a desiccated chicken breast. Since I don't relish a power saw ripping up my sternum, I guess I'll aspire to free range austerity.

Try out the new fad diet, called eating fewer calories. Surprise, surprise. A study out this last year said that all the diets—low carb, low fat, high protein, weight watchers, sex three times a day—were all the same. The only thing that mattered was the total caloric intake, no matter how you got it. Shocking. So I have it figured this way—I quit eating Wednesday morning completely, so that Saturday after rounds and cleaning up the office and seeing postop patients I can go to the Muzzle Loader and have the chicken fried steak, cream gravy, with wheat toast for health purposes. Since that meal has approximately 7,300 calories, depending on how much ketchup you put on the hash browns, three days of fasting are required to stay on budget. And a couple extra Lipitor.

Reduce whining. Whining causes heart attacks, cancer, and impotence. Studies have shown that (whenever anyone says studies have shown something, it is a lie for sure.) I'll get back to you on the references. Anyway. I took my son to the Muzzle Loader (Child Protective Services on line one), and along the way I saw a billboard for cosmetic facial procedures offered by radiologists, and then at the restaurant there was an ad in the paper from an ear, nose, and throat doctor in Bozeman for breast implants. I was explaining to my son that it is interesting that everyone wants the plastic surgery procedures that pay cash, but none of these guys competes with us for the pressure sores, infected wounds, or burns. He's a good kid, and he tried valiantly to look indignant for me, but basically he was tolerating my whining with one eye on the kitchen. Shut up and do your job, and leave the whining to the, well, whiners.

Participate in worthwhile charitable causes. I am going to continue my work with the Orthopedic Surgeons Literacy

Project. It takes a lot of time and patience, but when you see those big lugs (they are really muscular from pounding in those artificial hips and knees, and stuffing me in lockers in high school) put the "C" and the "A" and the "T" together for the first time, it can really choke you up.

Ignore traffic signals. I like to walk at night, and I would be long dead if I crossed the road on a green light with the little white walk figure lit up. At least three cars blow through an intersection in Billings *after* a light turns red, usually accelerating as if going really fast running the light somehow makes it less egregious. I've thought about carrying a paintball gun on walks with me and nailing the vehicles trying to kill me, but I'd likely get sued. So walking for me is like playing Call of Duty—32nd Street—everyone for themselves.

Another study, here it comes. People who are grateful and express it are happier. I want a chunk of that action, so here goes. I am grateful to all of you who take the time to write or tell me in person that you appreciate and enjoy what I write, and for all of you who tell me that I am inane and undignified and blasphemous and write goat mucous, I am grateful I have better taste than you. Happy New Year, and pass the olive oil.

Chapter 12
Body and Spirit

The threat of illness and death challenges our spiritual foundation like no other life experience. Does God heal us, are prayers answered, and what must we do for others are all imponderable questions.

~~~~~~~~~~~~~~~~~~~~~~~~~~~~~~~

As You Do Unto Others

The caller ID reads "Elliot", and as usual the conversation begins in mid-sentence. It may be from any of ten different threads (patients, hoops, kids, etc.), but as you know with long-time homies, it flows just fine.

"So our guy, I dunno, there could be infected bone under that flap."

"Our guy" completely smashed his lower leg and ankle on a construction job. The employer offered cash wages (discounted, naturally) so he wasn't annoyed with details like social security, withholding, and oh yeah, worker's comp. Our guy was spared reporting the income, and oh yeah, taxes. Works for all.

Almost. The only problem with that scenario is that if worker's comp doesn't know you exist, you aren't covered if you completely smash your lower leg and ankle. Oops.

He had two major reconstructions done in another town, but the overlying skin died, leaving the hardware exposed and infected. I took the rectus muscle from his abdomen, wrapped it around the carnage, and got Jim involved to sort out this rummage sale of bones.

My flap lives, but the bone narrative has a lot of chapters left. So every couple weeks I get a call from "Elliot". "Could fuse the thing through the calcaneus, but then he won't bend the ankle ever again. If we reconstruct it, we're back to plates and their problems." He's taken the guy to the OR three times now. Once the patient's ride was hours late--they had trouble raising money for gas. Instead of cancelling, Jim waited and did him at 7. He calls me, infectious disease, home health, the original surgeon, and in general spends a lot of time thinking about this person.

You've heard the expression "like a dog with a bone"? This is like a dog in scrubs with lots of little pieces of broken bones.

At no point in this process will he ever be paid a nickel. The patient has no job, no assets, and had already racked up fifty or sixty grand before he ever got to us. At no point in his determined musing on this man has Jim ever mentioned or expressed any concern about any of this.

When I did the muscle flap procedure, I asked my partner, Steve Grosso, to give me five hours on a Saturday to help. No sighs, no rolled eyes, just "sure."

Here's a multiple choice test: A 28 year old male is fleeing the scene of a liquor store robbery in a stolen TransAm. He misses a curve at 120 mph, and then attempts conjugal relations with a tree. His odds of having health insurance are a) 0% or b) what have you been smoking? The admitting trauma surgeon at SVH or BC may never operate on the guy, but he does get to call the neurosurgeon, orthopedist, plastic surgeon, and other

138

cranky specialists at three a.m. He then tries to get them to do their jobs for the next six weeks, while our patient blows mucous bubbles out of his tracheostomy. But again, they advocate for these sociopathic losers like it was their own kid.

Don't get me wrong, I certainly don't feel sorry for any of these guys. We make good money—not 54 foot trawler yacht money, but certainly 19 foot Sea Ray money. Frankly, I wouldn't do this, after 18 years of post-high school training, unless I did make good money. I'm not that good of a person.

But the greatest reward for me is that I get to know people like Jim and Steve and a whole lot of other providers who take great care of people who have nothing. I've seen doctors take good care of the indigent but with sanctimonious condescension. Not these folks. I know that it really matters to them whether this patient walks, and it matters whether he can bend his ankle.

In Matthew Chapter 25, Jesus speaks of having to account to The Big Guy about our actions. "Truly I tell you, whatever you did for one of the least of these brothers and sisters of mine, you did for me." I worry about that—are there patients being sent my way who are really celestial spies, checking to see if I am worthy or just faking it?

Maybe, maybe not. No sense taking chances.

Will God Heal Me When I Am Sick?

My surgical training included a rotation on pediatric cardiac surgery. One of the patients was Chelsea, a little cutie born with a badly malformed heart, and she was awaiting a transplant. Members of a "megachurch", the parents informed me that due to a prayer chain involving other large churches, over 600,000 persons were praying for Chelsea.

A few beds away was Kendra. She was a tiny, emaciated-looking offspring of a "crack mother". Kendra had had complicated open-heart surgery, and was struggling. No one was praying for Kendra.

Many questions troubled me. Would a prayer for Chelsea be a prayer for the death of the donor, another child? Would thousands of prayers help Chelsea recover, while Kendra died of heavenly neglect? Was it God's will that both these children suffer?

Does God give children leukemia?

Does God's will include letting your teenager die in a car crash?

Does God think that arthritis will make you a better person?

Will God heal you when you are sick?

After 25 years in surgery, I have no answers, but I am shaping some ideas.

Jesus had both earthly and heavenly parents. I do also. My earthly parents love me unconditionally and simply couldn't hurt me. I do the same for my children.

Is God's love any less devoted? Is God's love for you not absolute?

Would you break your daughter's arm to teach her something? Would God put a cancer in your brain? I can't believe that. I think that God loves you too much to hurt you.

God has given us the gift, and the curse, of self-determination. One particular human has helped us understand God's love.

Jesus, in the wilderness, suffered cold, hunger, and thirst. One of the reasons Jesus became human was to show us how to be human.

Jesus prayed as he faced death "Take this cup from me." Yet he died an agonizing death of bleeding and suffocation on the cross. Why didn't God save him? As a parent, I believe God suffered terribly, but both God and Jesus knew that to be human is to suffer at times, and ultimately to die. Sometimes we feel God has forgotten us as we suffer illness or loss. Even Jesus asked, "Why have you forsaken me?"

What will God do for you?

Those of you who have coached know that you can train your charges vigorously, drill them endlessly, and teach them all you know; you can give them your soul--yet you can never make a play on the field. God wants us to make the most of our humanity. That includes meeting the challenges of illness and injury when they occur. Through our prayers and our faith, we ask God to help us draw all our resources together to be healed--our friends, our family, all who pray for us, health care givers, and most of all, ourselves. God's love is what helps us do the best we can. Yet like any coach, I do not think God makes plays or changes the score. It is our life to live.

I was at Chelsea's bedside when she died after her second heart transplant. It was a brutally heartbreaking moment, yet there was a powerful sensation of great and gentle hands, reaching for and enveloping this weary baby, and drawing her ever so close. Kendra survived and went to a foster home, and I've always wondered about her, now 17.

God did not promise these children life, health, or even happiness. God's promise is that in life, or in death, we will never be alone.

Pizza or Prayer

The late spring rain lashed the hillside visible through the windows of the Surgical Intensive Care Unit. An ambulance was wailing its way to the emergency entrance. Inside was a 19 year-old man (boy?) who, as a passenger in a light pick-up truck, had been crushed when a cement truck had skidded sideways on the wet pavement just outside of town. Overturning, it fell upon him and the still trapped but quite dead driver.

As a surgeon in my third year of training, I was assigned for three months to the Surgical Intensive Care Unit (SICU) to increase my experience in caring for the most critically ill of patients. This included the care of trauma patients, one of whom was now being unloaded from the ambulance as I hurried down the stairway to the emergency department.

The well-choreographed trauma procedure assumed the rhythm of a long-running Broadway play. A tube was placed in the victim's windpipe to assure a stable airway, important here because of his misshapen and swollen head. A respiratory technician squeezed oxygen from a bag into the tube and to his lungs, which from the smashed appearance of his chest were likely to need help. His abdomen was distended, likely from blood lost from the liver or spleen. His pelvis moved inappropriately with palpation, suggesting its fracture. No maneuvers were required to appreciate the disruption of his femurs, which stuck angrily in pieces through the skin in his thighs.

Only intermittently were we able to obtain a blood pressure, despite the continuous administration of unmatched blood and salt solutions. The senior surgeon present made the decision to take him immediately to the operating room to try to control the worst of the internal bleeding. Just as quickly as this scene had begun, it ended as the entourage speeded toward the OR.

I returned to the SICU to prepare for his later arrival, although I did not believe he would be joining us. The severity of his injuries and his profound instability already were certainly poor indicators. As the nursing staff and I prepared for a stormy night, the nursing supervisor called to say that the patient's mother had arrived in the surgical waiting area. Since I, not on the operating team, was available, would I speak to the mother?

I don't care how hardened or cynical or tough you are, no doctor likes to bring bad news to a family, especially when it involves a child. It is the worst job in medicine. I could not see a way to duck this situation.

Mom was a small, trim woman with neat, wiry gray hair who rose quickly and greeted me with a firm handshake.

"I'm Janet Carella, Patrick's mother." I was surprised by her composure. There was concern but no tears, an almost businesslike manner.

I explained the nature and severity of his injuries, expressing particular concern for what looked like a major neurological insult to his brain. She asked questions appropriately and then

142

thanked me for the update. I didn't feel like she understood how bad it was.

"Mrs. Carella, your son has suffered devastating injuries, and his survival is very much in doubt."

"Doctor, I heard and understood you. My son will be okay if we all do our job." I thought that a strange comment.

Two hours later the surgeons brought Patrick to the SICU. They were apologetic, as he wasn't much more stable than before. They had removed his spleen and part of his liver to stop some of the bleeding. He hadn't been stable enough to do much else.
As nurses gathered him into our critical care embrace, I assessed the carnage. Beginning at the top, he had pressure bandages on several scalp lacerations I would need to close. We still had a harrowing trip to the CT scanner to assess his brain. His cervical spine would need x-rays. Tubes from his chest cavities were pouring out blood at an alarming rate. I was dubious that the intraabdominal bleeding was under control, as several drains placed around the liver seemed to be competing with the chest tubes for the bleeding title. He had a metal contraption holding his pelvis in place, and dressings where the open fracture sites on the legs had been washed out. At least I didn't have to look at the ends of the bones.

That night was awful. We poured blood and fluid and large doses of blood pressure raising drugs into him just to keep faint vital signs. We survived the trip to the CT scanner, barely, where we learned he had a major brain contusion. After all the bleeding and transfusions his blood would no longer clot, which made everything worse.

I shared the SICU duties with another resident. I worked 12 hours of a day and he worked the other 12 hours. I knew that I would leave at 7 a.m. the next day. I also knew that if could just keep Patrick alive until then, I wouldn't have to tell Patrick's mom that he was dead. I know that sounds weak on my part, but I think it had a lot to do with my efforts that night. At one point we lost his blood pressure altogether, and I stepped out to ask her to come in to be with him at the end.

"Keep working", she said, "this isn't the end." I was on the verge of annoyance. I told her that we had done all we could and that his injuries were greater than his resources to fight them.

"God is with him now, and he is also with you and your team. I have faith in Patrick and in you, even if you don't."

Frankly, she intimidated me, and I returned to work. At one point I picked up the chest tube containers full of blood and hung them from IV poles, pouring the thin red fluid back into Patrick because we had run out of blood products. Anything to get to 7 a.m..

At midnight, a wonderful thing happened. A delivery man stepped into the ICU with an enormous pizza box. We asked each other who had ordered the pizza, no one had. We reluctantly told him we had not made an order, but he told us that it came from Carella's pizza, free of charge. Mrs. Carella of Carella's Pizza!! No one had made the connection to the well-known local pizzeria.

It was a glorious creation--layers of juicy meats, succulent vegetables, delirious cheeses. The stressed and ravenous crew inhaled this feast of saturated fat as soldiers under siege.

Grease dripping from my chin, I went to the waiting area to thank Mrs. Carella. She held a bemused expression.

"You're most welcome. In fact, each night that Patrick is here you will receive a similar pizza."

Finally 7 a.m. arrived. Every trick I knew to keep someone alive I had tried twice. My partner Scott arrived and surveyed the wreckage.

"Great. Now I'm stuck with this guy dying on me." His resentment was not subtle. I left gratefully, but knowing I would not see Patrick again.

Sleep that day was fitful. It is hard to sleep during the day, much less after a harrowing day of probably futile efforts. The grotesque nature of his injuries bothered me. It could have

144

been me or anyone else in that little truck. I had a bizarre dream about Mrs. Carella, using pizzas as coins, popping them into a big machine to keep her son alive.

My bleary eyes popped open that evening when I saw Patrick's bed still occupied in the SICU. Scott had an evil grin on his face. He had doubled the drugs, tripled the blood products. He had used all of his wiles and more. "Man, that mom shakes me up. She is convinced he will be well again. Sorry partner, but you can tell her she's wrong." He then wiped a rivulet of grease off his chin.

That night I spent a few hours reassembling Patrick's scalp. I turned the TV in his room to a late NBA playoff game, and settled into a not unpleasant rhythm of trimming and sewing. The television announcer exclaimed loudly after a fast break culminated in a thunderous jam, and Patrick startled. I reflexively told him to hold still, and then I realized that he had shown his first sign of meaningful neurological activity.

Other than suturing, I was watching the clock—10 p.m., 11, and then yes! On time and on cue the pizza man arrived. This pie, if possible, was even more marvelous and unhealthy than the last. We toasted Patrick's health with caffeinated coke.

I also had an extended visit with Mrs. Carella. I told her about the good news of Patrick's response, which (again annoyingly so) didn't seem to surprise her. I obtained consent for the next day's operations, which would include reopening his abdomen to remove the packs around his liver, and also procedures to stabilize his femur fractures with metal rods. I spoke of the looming threats of infection, blood clots, and pneumonia. Then she startled me again.

"I want you to know that I am praying for you. I have asked God to place the healing powers of Christ in your hands and in the hands of the staff. These operations will repair his body parts, as you did with his scalp, but it will take God's power to heal him."

I mumbled some thanks for the pizza and departed, feeling uncomfortable. This business is a lot easier when it is not personal.

The next night (Canadian bacon and pineapple) was tough after all the surgery. I think all the transfusions had caught up with his lungs, as especially platelets can cause reactions that impair breathing. We adjusted the respirator with the help of a lung specialist and limped through the night. Scott did a great job during the day (southwestern taco supreme) to stabilize Patrick.

The following evening marked three special events. First of all, we gave Patrick no blood products of any kind. Secondly, a nurse asked him to squeeze her hand and he did—a major indicator of neurological function. And finally, Mrs. Carella actually listened to me when I told her to go home and get some rest. I did this with some trepidation, as I was fearful it might affect pizza delivery. Fear not, it arrived, ever caloric and wonderful.

The days ahead saw incremental but noticeable improvement in Patrick. After ten days of mechanical ventilation (a prison I can't comprehend) he was extubated and breathing on his own. He croaked a few words. His battered kidney function rallied. His yellow jaundice, present from liver trauma and all the loose blood in his body, cleared.

I actually told Mrs. Carella that I thought Patrick would survive now. She smiled, condescendingly I thought.

"If you had had faith from the beginning, you could have spared yourself all those doubtful thoughts."

Finally the day arrived when it became apparent that Patrick was stable enough to leave the SICU. He would transfer to a general trauma patient floor, then on to rehabilitation. He would need to learn to walk again, and his brain function had a ways to go as well. At 7 a.m., as Scott and I were together at shift change, we watched a highly emotional moment as Patrick passed through the doors of the SICU alive and recovering. As I took deep breaths, I noticed that my scrub pants were rather snug around my abdomen. I mourned the midnight pizzas, but perhaps it was for the best.

146

The next two months passed quickly, as time seems to compress during intense experiences. I was writing in a chart when the automatic door swung open, and there was Mrs. Carella. With her was a tall young man on crutches, braces on his legs, and short but thick hair. He deliberately made his way toward me at his mother's direction. He then took a large, flat box from her.

"I don't know you, but my mom says that your team deserves at least one more of these." A pizza! A deluxe supreme combo pull-out-all-the-stops monster! The familiar aroma filled us with drooling gluttony.

"Patrick," I said, "knowing that this pizza was coming each night I believe saved your life."

Mrs. Carella stepped forward.

"Son," she said softly but with her characteristic steel, "I am so ever grateful to those of you who helped bring Patrick through. I hope you learned a great deal taking care of him. But for this tragedy to have meaning, you must understand that the Lord Jesus Christ healed him."

I'd had about enough.

"If you're so sure," I retorted, "why did you bribe us with that pizza every night?

"The Lord expects us to use all of our gifts," she replied calmly. "One of mine is a pizza parlor."

With that, she and Patrick slowly but steadily left us.

Was it the pizza or was it the prayer? Perhaps the Lord works in mysterious ways, and some of them are round.

Made in the USA
San Bernardino, CA
01 January 2013